New
Charleston
CUISINE

50 defining dishes from the Holy City's top kitchens

New
Charleston
CUISINE

50 defining dishes from the Holy City's top kitchens

HANNA RASKIN

EVENING POST
BOOKS

Published by
Evening Post Books
Charleston, South Carolina

Copyright © 2017 The Post and Courier
All rights reserved.
First edition

Designer: Gill Guerry

First printing 2017
Printed in the United States of America

A CIP catalog record for this book has been applied
for from the Library of Congress.

ISBN: 978-1-929647-33-0

Table of Contents

Introduction

This cookbook represents the first-ever compilationt of signature recipes from Charleston's leading restaurant chefs, with four James Beard Foundation award winners among them.

Within these pages, you'll find the secrets to Sean Brock's benne salsa, which Southern Foodways Alliance director John T. Edge once credited with provoking the epiphany that the partition between Old and New South has crumbled. You'll learn how to make Mike Lata's smoked oysters, characterized by Tasting Table as the long-awaited salvation of saltine crackers. Here, too, are recipes for the pickled shrimp, pea-and-peanut salad and duck-and-oyster rice pie that serve as climactic moments in the epic food stories told by visitors to wistful folks back home.

So in its substance, this book is original and unique. But in its celebration of Charleston's contemporary dining scene, it assuredly is not.

In the year prior to this book's publication, Charleston was named one of the world's greatest eating cities by magazines including *Food & Wine*, *Conde Nast Traveler* and *Travel & Leisure*. At this moment, it seems as though diners' affection and admiration for the area's restaurants is boundless. Is it something in the water?

No. At least, not directly. It's in the wreckfish and triggerfish, the shrimp and blue crab along with the people who catch, prepare and serve them. It's in the Jimmy Red corn and the people who distill it. It's in the field peas, tomatoes, eggplants, okra and mustard greens, as well as the people who grow them.

All of that doesn't easily travel, either through space or time. It's impossible for a home cook living in Indonesia or a party host in 2029 to fully know the culinary spirit of a city that's captivated millions of diners. Hospitality and style are as fleeting as the peak of peach season.

But that doesn't mean interested eaters can't conjure at least a taste of what makes Charleston so special right now. Charleston has been hailed for its food and drink for centuries, but the current moment is exceptional by any measure. Every chef who contributed a recipe to this cookbook was asked to come up with a dish that captures it.

This is the second time that *The Post and Courier* has published a cookbook. Fifty years before the launch of this project, The Evening Post Publishing Company asked food editor Charlotte Walker to put together *The Post-Courier Cookbook,* a spiral-bound recipe collection that started with Basic White Bread and ended with Porcupine Spread.

Unlike some of the best-known recipes from the best-known local cookbook, the Junior

League of Charleston's *Charleston Receipts* ("this book makes no attempt to compete," Walker clarified in her introduction), Porcupine Spread didn't call for wild game. Instead, it was a cream cheese-and-deviled ham ball, coated in crushed pretzels and decorated with green olives. Did I mention the book appeared in 1966?

Walker was right. Her cookbook wasn't timeless or intensely regional, in the way of *Charleston Receipts*. "*The Post-Courier Cookbook* is general, with major emphasis on new developments in food preparation techniques," she wrote. In other words, it's impossible to cook from the book (which is available in digital form at post-andcourier.com), and not be struck by its reliance on mayonnaise, frozen orange juice and bouillon cubes.

New Charleston Cuisine is general, with major emphasis on new developments. In honor of *The Post-Courier Cookbook*'s silver anniversary, it was designed to function as an edible time capsule, with recipes that would forevermore jolt eaters back to 2016.

For that reason, there are repetitions and redundancies here, which we anticipated when we first solicited contributions to this series. As the invitation sent to chefs said, "The idea here is not to rehash the classics … I'd expect to see more shishito peppers than shrimp paste." And we did see shishitos, along with multiple recipes for crab cakes, falafel and ceviche. Rather than disrupt the historical record, we kept all of them, just as *The Post-Courier Cookbook* ran recipe after recipe for dishes made with gelatin.

Already, 2016 seems like a long time ago. Although that's when these recipes began appearing in *The Post and Courier*'s food section on a weekly basis, the restaurant landscape isn't the same as when we started. Readers who keep up with area restaurants will find recipes attributed to restaurants that are no longer in business, and chefs who've lost their jobs since participating in this project. In fact, it's quite likely more shifts and shuffles will rearrange the Charleston restaurant picture after this text goes to print.

After all, the city's restaurants are always changing. No wonder Charleston is cause for excitement.

A final note: These recipes were developed for restaurants and haven't been tested for home use. What we can guarantee is the dishes accurately reflect today's Charleston and the talented chefs with whom we're lucky to share it. Please enjoy.

Hanna Raskin
Food editor and chief critic,
The Post and Courier

Cannonborough – Elliotborough

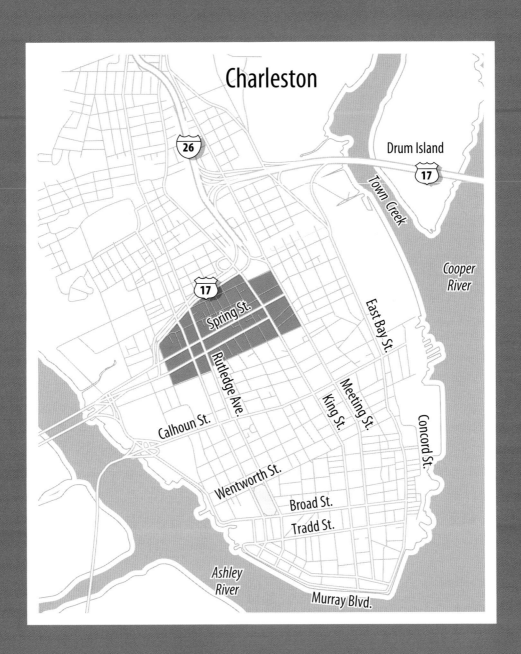

Charleston

Drum Island

Town Creek

Cooper River

East Bay St.

Spring St.

Rutledge Ave.

Meeting St.

King St.

Concord St.

Calhoun St.

Wentworth St.

Broad St.

Tradd St.

Ashley River

Murray Blvd.

Shrimp Bog Rice

Chefs participating in this project were asked to prioritize contemporary over classic, but Hominy Grill's awareness of local culinary history is part of what makes the Cannonborough-Elliotborough restaurant so special. Stehling says of this recipe, "I think it indicative of what Hominy does, making a classic part of our modern lives, but it's also a snapshot of what Charleston restaurant cooking has aspired to become: fresh, local and heirloom."

RECIPE BY Robert Stehling

1 tablespoon whole butter	½ cup diced celery	1 bay leaf
1 cup quartered and sliced andouille sausage	½ cup diced red bell pepper	3½ cups shrimp stock
1 cup diced yellow onion	½ cup diced green bell pepper	1 pound raw shrimp, peeled and split lengthwise, three-quarters
½ teaspoon minced garlic	1 cup Carolina gold rice middlins (see cook's note)	of the way toward the tail end

Directions:

In a 4-quart saucepan, brown sausage in butter over medium-high heat; remove sausage and set aside. Add onions to pan and saute until they start to brown.

Reduce heat to medium; add garlic and celery to pan. Cook until celery is tender. Increase heat to medium-high and add peppers to pan. Cook until they start to soften, about 2-3 minutes.

Add rice to pan. Turn down heat to medium-low and saute rice and vegetable mixture for 2 minutes.

Add the browned sausage and bay leaf to the pan, and stir in about 1 cup of stock. Stir vigorously to break up the starches, and then add the rest of the stock in stages, reserving ½ cup. When rice is nearly cooked, stir in shrimp and remaining ½ cup of stock. Bring to a boil, turn off heat and cover. Let sit covered for 5 minutes, or until shrimp are cooked. Remove bay leaf before serving.

COOK'S NOTE:

Middlins, or rice grits, are available through Anson Mills.
Check with your favorite gourmet grocer or order from **ansonmills.com.**

GRACE BEAHM ALFORD

Yu Xiang (Fish-Fragrant) Summer Vegetables

There isn't any fish in Sichuan fish-fragrant sauce, one of almost two dozen complex sauces considered essential to the provincial Chinese cuisine. But because it features seasonings often paired with seafood, the sauce makes any dish reminiscent of fish.

It's also been suggested that the sauce's strong flavors could help disguise fish that's no longer fresh.

That's not the case at Xiao Bao Biscuit, where Walker combines the sauce with locally grown tomatoes and eggplants to make what he describes as "almost Chinese-Italian food."

According to Walker, this dish is "garlicky, savory, simple and delicious."

RECIPE BY Joshua Walker

4 tomatoes
2 tablespoons peanut oil
2 eggplants (Louisiana green and Japanese purple varieties are recommended)

⅓ cup garlic, chopped
⅓ cup Fresno pepper, fermented
½ cup mapo paste (see cook's note)
2 tablespoons sugar
2½ tablespoons mushroom soy sauce

1⅔ tablespoons Chinkiang vinegar (see cook's note)
1⅔ tablespoons chili oil

Directions:

Preheat oven to 250 degrees. Cut tomatoes in quarters. Toss with oil and bake on a sheet pan for 3 hours. Set aside.

Cut eggplants into rectangular planks. Cook over medium heat in a dry cast-iron pan. Cook skin side up and flip when you achieve a nice char on the bottom.

Cook for one more minute or until eggplant is soft.

Mix together sauce (garlic through chili oil) in a medium-sized bowl. Pour into a saucepan and heat over low heat, stirring constantly, until just warm.

Return sauce to bowl along with tomatoes and eggplants. Toss thoroughly before plating.

COOK'S NOTE:

Mapo, or fermented fava bean paste, sometimes called "dou ban jiang" and Chinkiang vinegar are sold at Asian markets.

GRACE BEAHM ALFORD

Pea-and-Peanut Salad

When Deihl and Cook opened Artisan Meat Share, they planned to adjust side items seasonally. The now-closed charcuterie shop offered specials on a daily basis, but its customers made clear they wouldn't stand for the suspension of this Southern salad, which Cook likes alongside a porchetta sandwich.

RECIPE BY Craig Deihl (left) and Bob Cook

PEA-and-PEANUT SALAD

2 cups English peas, blanched
1 cup quartered radish

1 cup hard-roasted peanuts
¼ cup Green Goddess dressing

Salt and pepper to taste

Directions:

In a medium-sized bowl, add all ingredients and mix well. Season with salt and pepper.

GREEN GODDESS DRESSING

⅓ cup chopped parsley
¼ cup chopped chives
2 tablespoons chopped tarragon
¼ cup chopped basil
1 tablespoon chopped anchovy

1 teaspoon chopped garlic
2 tablespoons extra virgin olive oil
⅓ cup mayonnaise
3 tablespoons sour cream
½ tablespoon sugar

1 tablespoon plus 1 teaspoon poppy seeds
1 teaspoon lemon juice
Salt and pepper to taste

Directions:

In a food processor, combine parsley, chives, tarragon, basil, anchovy, garlic and olive oil. Blend until pureed. In separate bowl, combine mayonnaise, sour cream, sugar, poppy seeds and lemon juice; mix well.

Combine the mayonnaise mixture with the herb mixture and incorporate evenly. Season with salt and pepper to taste. Store in an airtight container and refrigerate until ready to use. Will keep for up to six weeks.

HARD-ROASTED PEANUTS

Preheat oven to 350 degrees. Evenly distribute peanuts onto a cookie sheet and bake for 20 minutes.

WADE SPEES

Fusilli Pasta with Butternut Squash and Duck Sausage

Assuming you're as handy with a grinder as a gun, this recipe from Ken Vedrinski might be just the thing to remember come duck season. But making your own duck sausage is by no means a prerequisite: Any kind of Italian sausage will do.

RECIPE BY Ken Vedrinski

2 ounces unsalted butter
12 large fusilli pasta shells
4 cups duck Italian ground sausage or substitute Italian sausage
¼ cup chopped flat-leaf parsley

2 cups of 1-inch diced butternut squash
1½ cups freshly grated Parmesan cheese
Kosher salt and black pepper

1 cup packed blanched, chopped broccoli spigerello (or any other winter greens except collards), squeezed of excess liquid

Directions:

Melt the butter in a small saucepan over low heat. Increase the heat to medium and cook the butter until the milk solids brown, 3-4 minutes. Remove immediately and set aside.

Fill a pot with heavily salted water over high heat. Add the pasta and cook until al dente, 7-10 minutes. Drain, but do not rinse.

Saute the sausage in a skillet over medium heat until cooked through. Using a slotted spoon, transfer the sausage to a large bowl, reserving the fat in the skillet. Increase the heat to medium-high, add the squash and cook, stirring frequently, until tender, 8 to 10 minutes. Add the greens to the skillet and cook until wilted. Toss vegetables with pasta; top with cheese and parsley. Salt and pepper to taste.

GRACE BEAHM ALFORD

Charred Okra with Spiced Tomato Gravy

The Grocery serves charcuterie and steak tartare, but the downtown restaurant has earned a reputation as a vegetarian haven, partly on the strength of exceptional dishes such as this customer favorite. The contrasting okra textures and slap of vinegar make a garden-variety combination special.

RECIPE BY Kevin Johnson

CHARRED OKRA WITH SPICED TOMATO GRAVY

1 pound small okra, halved lengthwise
1 cup buttermilk
1 cup stone-ground cornmeal, seasoned with salt and cayenne pepper to taste
Vegetable oil for frying

½ pound okra, sliced into ½-inch thick rounds
1 small yellow onion, julienned very thin
8 sprigs oregano leaves, picked and minced
3 tablespoons olive oil

Salt and pepper to taste
6 ounces cherry tomatoes, halved
12 sprigs Italian parsley, leaves picked
6 to 8 ounces spiced tomato gravy
10 to 12 each pickled okra, slivered
3 to 4 ounces cotija cheese, finely grated

Directions:

Heat a large Dutch oven with enough vegetable oil to fry okra. Toss halved okra with buttermilk in a bowl until coated. Drain off any excess buttermilk. Coat okra with cornmeal. Fry okra in oil at 360 degrees until golden and crispy. Remove from oil; drain; let rest briefly on a paper towel-lined pan.

Combine okra rounds, onion and oregano in a mixing bowl. Drizzle with olive oil and season with salt and pepper.

Heat a cast-iron skillet over high heat until very hot. Arrange okra rounds in skillet in a single layer. Cook for 3 to 4 minutes without stirring to get a nice char. Shake pan carefully and cook for another 2 to 3 minutes. Okra is ready when nicely charred and tender, but not soft.

Quickly combine fried okra, charred okra, cherry tomatoes and parsley in a mixing bowl. You can either plate it individually or on a large platter to share. Either way, place a puddle of warmed tomato gravy on plate. Top with okra mixture. Garnish with a few spoonfuls of slivered pickled okra, and sprinkle with cotija cheese.

PICKLED OKRA

1 cup white vinegar
½ cup water
1 tablespoon salt
1 tablespoon sugar

1 tablespoon mustard seed, toasted
2 teaspoons fennel seed, toasted
½ teaspoon red pepper flakes, toasted

½ jalapeno pepper, thinly sliced
15 to 20 whole okra

WADE SPEES

Directions:

Bring all ingredients, except okra, to a boil. Pour vinegar mixture over okra. Chill and store in the refrigerator, or pack into a sterilized jar; seal and process in boiling water for 15 minutes.

SPICED TOMATO GRAVY

4 medium-size tomatoes, halved and cored
Salt and pepper to taste
1 small yellow onion, thinly sliced
1 tablespoon minced ginger
½ teaspoon turmeric
1 teaspoon paprika
1 tablespoon cumin seed, toasted
1 tablespoon coriander seed, toasted
2 teaspoons fennel seed, toasted
1 teaspoon chili powder
Small pinch of red pepper flakes
6 sprigs oregano
3 tablespoons sherry vinegar

Directions:

Preheat broiler. Place tomatoes, cut side down in an ovenproof dish. Season with salt and pepper; broil tomatoes until deeply charred, very soft and seeping juice. Remove tomatoes from oven and place, along with juice, in a blender. Add all remaining ingredients, puree in batches if necessary. Season with salt and pepper. If it is too acidic, you can whisk in a few tablespoons of olive oil. Use right away or chill and use within 5 days.

Raspberry Pistachio Pinkie Print Cookies

This classic cookie is so easy to make that you barely need a recipe. In fact, it's a perfect preparation to commit to memory, and Carrie-Ann Bach of Brown's Court Bakery has supplied the measurements and method worth knowing. Although this version calls for pistachios and raspberry jam, once you've mastered the basics, you might start wiggling your pinkie whenever you have an interesting preserve in the pantry.

RECIPE BY Carrie-Ann Bach

1 cup soft butter	¼ teaspoon salt	1 cup raspberry jam
½ cup powdered sugar	2 cups all-purpose flour	
2 teaspoons vanilla extract	1 cup raw pistachios, finely chopped	

Directions:

Preheat oven to 325 degrees.

Cream butter and sugar in a stand mixer with paddle attachment for 2 minutes. Using a rubber spatula, scrape down the sides of the mixing bowl. Add vanilla and salt; mix on low until incorporated. Scrape down the sides of the bowl, add all-purpose flour and mix on low until cookie dough comes together.

Scoop dough into tablespoon-sized balls. Roll each cookie in chopped pistachios and arrange on a baking sheet.

Using your finger, make an indent in the center of each cookie. Fill the indent with raspberry jam. Bake until edges are golden brown, or about 10-15 minutes.

Pickled Shrimp

Aleppo has lately been in the news for reasons other than its namesake peppers, which is why the city's best-known delicacy is no longer available: The Syrian civil war has put an end to Aleppo pepper production. Spice merchants warn that anything labeled as Aleppo pepper is either counterfeit or too old to use. Among the spice cognoscenti, Maras pepper from Turkey has emerged as a favorite substitute, but a blend of cayenne and paprika also will work in this pickling liquid from Kevin Getzewich.

RECIPE BY Kevin "Getz" Getzewich

COURT BOUILLON

12 quarts water
2 quarts white wine
3 onions, sliced
3 celery ribs, sliced

3 carrots, sliced
1 fennel head, sliced
2 tablespoons black pepper
2 tablespoons coriander

3 lemons, sliced
1 cup salt

Directions:

Add all ingredients to a large pot over high heat. Once mixture reaches a boil, reduce heat and simmer for 30 minutes. Turn off heat; steep for 1 hour. Strain mixture and return liquid to pot.

PICKLING LIQUID

2½ quarts water
1 quart white wine vinegar
1 quart cider vinegar
Zest and juice of 4 lemons
Zest and juice of 4 oranges

2 cups sugar
2 tablespoons coriander
2 tablespoons mustard seed
2 tablespoon red pepper flakes
2 tablespoons black pepper

1 tablespoon Aleppo pepper
1 tablespoon smoked paprika
2 bay leaves
⅔ cup salt

Directions:

Add all ingredients to a large pot over high heat. Bring to a boil. Turn off heat; steep for 1 hour. Strain and return mixture to pot.

WADE SPEES

SHRIMP

5 pounds shrimp, peeled and deveined
3 cloves garlic, sliced
1 shallot, sliced

Directions:

Add shrimp to pot containing court bouillon; partially cook over medium-high heat, about 1-2 minutes. Transfer shrimp from pot to sealable container using a slotted spoon. Top with garlic and shallot. Pour pickling liquid over mixture and close the container. Refrigerate overnight. Remove bay leaves before serving.

Peruvian Ceviche

Of all the countries with a ceviche tradition, it's possible none of them are prouder of the raw fish dish than Peru. Some food historians believe people living along the present-day Peruvian coast thousands of years ago may have pioneered the technique of curing fish in fruit juice.

But even if ceviche originated in far-off Polynesia, as also has been suggested, it's now a cherished Peruvian food. In tribute to Peru's distinctive ceviche style, Amalia Scatena includes potatoes in her uncooked interpretation of flounder.

RECIPE BY Amalia Scatena

16 ounces flounder (or any flaky white fish)	¼ cup water	1 cup jicama
3 teaspoons kosher salt, plus more salt for finishing	2 tablespoons olive oil	2 avocados
6 limes, juiced	½ taro root	3 teaspoons shallots
	2 quarts sunflower oil	3 teaspoons jalapeno
	1 large sweet potato	½ cup cilantro

Directions:

Dice flounder, or any other white, lean and flaky fish such as triggerfish or red snapper, into ⅜-inch cubes. Salt with kosher salt. Combine lime juice, water and olive oil. Add salted fish to lime juice mixture; refrigerate for 3 hours. Using a mandolin, slice taro root to ¹⁄₁₆-inch thickness.

In a medium, high-sided pot, heat sunflower oil to 250 degrees. Once the oil is heated, drop taro slices into pot; cook until slices are crispy and slightly golden brown. Remove taro slices from oil; place them on a paper towel-lined plate and salt to taste. Cool. Bring medium pot of water to boil over high heat. Peel sweet potato and dice into ⅜-inch cubes. Blanch sweet potato until al dente. Cool. Keeping vegetables in separate piles, dice jicama and avocados into ⅜-inch cubes. Dice shallots and jalapenos into ⅛-inch cubes. Toss flounder with sweet potato, jicama, shallots, jalapenos and ¼ cup of cilantro. Divide into 8 portions. Garnish with avocado and remaining cilantro. Serve with taro chips.

MICHAEL PRONZATO

Smoked Oysters

I f there is one dish without which this book would be incomplete, it's The Ordinary's smoked oysters, which play an outsized role in so many visitors' dining memories of Charleston. Praised repeatedly in the national press, the dish arose from Mike Lata's attempt to recapture a California campfire experience.

"Success finally came when we ditched the pre-shucked jug oysters from Virginia, instead using the premium oysters that we serve on the half shell at the restaurant," Lata says. "I find that one of the remarkable things about this dish is the texture of the finished oyster."

RECIPE BY Mike Lata

12 saltine crackers	1 dozen fresh oysters	2 teaspoons minced shallots
1 tablespoon unsalted butter, melted	2 to 3 cups rock salt	1 teaspoon finely chopped chives
¼ teaspoon Old Bay seasoning	1 cup hickory chips, soaked in cold water	1 tablespoon fresh lemon juice
½ cup crème fraîche		1 tablespoon extra-virgin olive oil
¼ teaspoon finely grated lemon zest	1 tablespoon finely chopped heart of celery, leaves included	Hot sauce, for serving

Directions:

Preheat the oven to 375 degrees. Place the saltine crackers on a parchment-lined baking sheet. Brush both sides with melted butter and bake until golden brown, about 5 minutes. Remove from oven and immediately sprinkle with Old Bay seasoning. Let cool.

Whisk together crème fraîche and lemon zest and refrigerate. Prepare a charcoal grill. While the grill heats, partially shuck the oysters, removing the top shell but leaving the oyster attached to the bottom shell. Fill a pie tin with an even layer of rock salt (make sure it's a pie tin that you don't mind getting dirty) and nestle the oysters into the rock salt so they are level.

When the coals are smoldering, push to one side of the grill then scatter the soaked wood chips over the top. Replace the grill grate and set the pie tin on the side of the grill, away from the coals. Cover and smoke at 150 degrees for 15 minutes, until the oysters plump and the edges start to curl. When cool enough to handle, shuck oysters completely into a bowl. Gently fold in celery, shallots, chives, lemon juice and olive oil. Cover and chill for at least 30 minutes or up to overnight. Serve with saltines, crème fraîch and hot sauce.

MICHAEL PRONZATO

Smoked Beef Tartare

At the outset of this cookbook project, it seemed dangerously likely that half of the contributors would come up with steak tartare preparations: The raw beef dish is currently so popular that even seafood-focused restaurants take pride in their renditions.

But Greg Garrison's version is unique in its use of smoke. At Prohibition, it's smoked to order and served under a glass cloche. Garrison says, "If you do not wish to purchase a smoking gun, you can smoke this on your grill." Whew.

RECIPE BY Greg Garrison

16 anchovies, chopped	2 cups ketchup	Zest of 1 lemon
½ cup capers, chopped	2 tablespoons lemon juice	Wood chips for grilling
3 tablespoons Dijon mustard	1 tablespoon hot sauce	1 pound lean grass-fed ribeye
3 egg yolks	¼ cup Worcestershire sauce	Sea salt
½ red onion, finely diced	2 cups garlic oil	Pickles and potato chips, for serving
¼ cup parsley, chopped	3 tablespoons sliced chives	

Directions:

Combine all dressing ingredients (anchovies through lemon zest) and refrigerate overnight.

Soak wood chips in water for 30 minutes. Drain. If using a charcoal grill, place wet chips directly on coals. For a gas grill, add chips to a smoker box or arrange in a loose foil pouch situated near a burner.

Remove any fat and connective tissue from the ribeye. Dice the meat into ⅛-inch cubes.

Place the beef in a nonreactive heat-proof vessel. Place that vessel over another heat-proof vessel filled with ice. Heat the grill until the chips start to smoke. Close the grill; smoke for 5 minutes.

Season smoked beef with sea salt to taste. Mix with ¼ cup of dressing. Divide beef into four equal portions and serve with pickles and potato chips.

MICHAEL PRONZATO

Bourbon Salted Caramel Cheesecake with Pralines

When Mitterer learned this cookbook was supposed to capture the Charleston food scene at this particular moment, a few ingredients immediately sprang to mind. Mitterer, who operates two bakery locations and supplies the sweets for countless weddings, is living in a salted caramel world. Additionally, she says, "bourbon, pecans and pistachios are king."

RECIPE BY Lauren Mitterer

1½ cups graham cracker crumbs
¼ cup sugar
6 tablespoons butter, room temperature
6 (8-ounce) packages cream cheese, room temperature

1½ cups sugar
1½ teaspoons vanilla extract
Pinch of salt
6 large eggs

¾ cup purchased salted caramel sauce, such as Jeni's Splendid Ice Cream's Salty Caramel Sauce or cook's preference, divided use
2 tablespoons bourbon
12 pralines, chopped

Directions:

Preheat oven to 350 degrees. Combine graham cracker crumbs, sugar and butter in bowl of a food processor or stand mixer. Blend until crumbs stick together. Press crumbs onto the bottom of a 10-inch springform pan with 3-inch-high sides. If an outer edge of crust is desired, press crumbs up 2 inches on the sides. Bake crust for 10 minutes. Cool.

Reduce oven temperature to 300 degrees.

In the bowl of a mixer with a paddle attachment, mix cream cheese until soft. Add the sugar, vanilla and salt; mix on low until very smooth. Remove the bowl from the mixer; scrape the sides of the bowl. Return the bowl to the mixer.

Slowly add eggs just until blended,

stopping occasionally to scrape sides of bowl. Carefully add and fold ½ cup of salted caramel sauce and bourbon into the mixture. Pour batter into crust.

Wrap foil around the outside of cheesecake pan. Place a sheet tray or larger pan underneath the wrapped cheesecake. Slowly add water around the cheesecake to create a water bath approximately 2 inches deep.

Carefully place the cheesecake in the oven. Bake until its center is set and the rest of the cake has a uniform jiggle, at least 50 minutes.

Start checking the cake after 30 minutes. If the top gets too dark, gently cover with foil. Remove cake from the oven as well as the water bath pan. Cool to room temperature,

MARLENA SLOSS

and then cool completely in the refrigerator.
When ready to remove from the pan, gently run a knife around the outside edge of the cheesecake and unlock the springform.

Cover the top with ¼ cup of caramel sauce and chopped pralines. Cut and serve from the bottom pan or carefully slide a cardboard cake circle underneath.

Togarashi Cheesecake

I t's not just the pastry that's deconstructed in this reinterpretation of a classic cheesecake from Hahn: The recipe also is considerably more free-form than most. In other words, Hahn prefers for each home cook to determine how this dessert ought to come together: "Let your creative side take over and show you the way."

So the amount and arrangement of pastry, crunch and fruit topping on each plate is up to you, although Hahn does recommend scattering sesame seeds as a finishing touch.

RECIPE BY Emily Hahn

1 lime	1 cup sugar	2 tablespoons cornstarch
1 orange	2 teaspoons togarashi spice	Pinch of salt
16 ounces softened cream cheese	4 tablespoons milk	2 eggs, beaten

Directions:

Preheat oven to 300 degrees.

Zest and juice the lime and orange into the bowl of a stand mixer with a paddle attachment. Add cream cheese, sugar and togarashi to the bowl. Beat on high for 3 minutes. In a separate bowl, make a slurry by whisking together the milk, cornstarch and salt. Whisk beaten eggs into the slurry. Add slurry to the cream cheese mixture; beat on high for 3 minutes, making sure to scrape the sides of the bowl.

Pour batter into a lined 9x9-inch pan and bake until set, approximately 12-15 minutes.

CRUNCH

1 quart graham cracker crumbs	1 tablespoon toasted white sesame seeds, ground	3 tablespoons brown sugar
1 tablespoon tahini paste		1 cup melted butter

Directions:

Preheat oven to 325 degrees. Process graham cracker crumbs, tahini paste, ground sesame seeds and brown sugar in a Robot Coupe or food processor until smooth.

Slowly add the melted butter until the mixture takes on the consistency of hard wet sand. Pack mixture onto a baking sheet and bake for approximately 30 minutes or until golden brown. Let cool for 1 hour before serving.

GRACE BEAHM ALFORD

FRUIT TOPPING

1 lime	¼ cup local honey	3 kiwi, cleaned and sliced
1 teaspoon grated fresh ginger	1 pint ripe strawberries	

Directions:

Juice and zest lime into a mixing bowl. Add remaining ingredients. Mix together, set aside.

Harleston Village

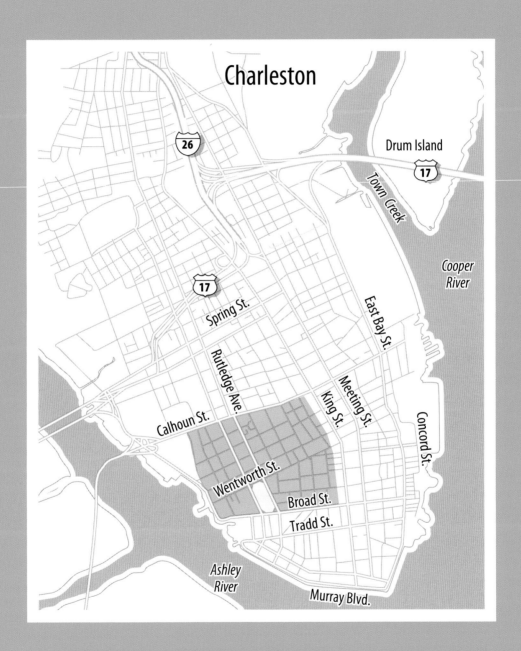

Falafel

From his perch at The Watch atop The Restoration hotel, Anderson had ample opportunity to survey the Charleston culinary scene, and he concluded it was short on Middle Eastern cooking. "Falafel is harder to find in a city like Charleston," Anderson says. "I feel that our twist on the original is a great addition to the varied and delicious foods served around town."

The twists include doing away with the pita wrap, substituting Greek yogurt tzatziki for tahini sauce and adding feta cheese.

RECIPE by Chad Anderson

1¼ cup dried chickpeas
2 garlic cloves, finely chopped
¾ cup finely chopped onion
½ cup chopped fresh cilantro
¼ cup chopped fresh flat-leaf parsley

1 teaspoon fine sea salt
¾ teaspoon ground cumin
½ teaspoon ground coriander
½ teaspoon black pepper
½ teaspoon baking soda
¼ teaspoon cayenne

About 6 cups vegetable oil (48 fluid ounces)
Tzatziki sauce and feta cheese for serving

DIRECTIONS:

To reconstitute chickpeas, put them in a bowl and cover by 2 inches with cold water. Leave bowl at room temperature for at least 12 hours. Drain well in colander.

Puree chickpeas with all remaing ingredients except oil in a food processor until smooth as possible, about 2 minutes. Spread puree in a 15x10x1-inch baking pan and let dry, uncovered, for 1 hour.

Scoop 2 tablespoons of puree onto a long sheet of wax paper, then press into a 2-inch wide patty. (Pressing the puree will help the patty hold together when frying.) Make a small hole in center of patty with tip of your pinkie finger (to help it cook evenly).

Make more patties in same manner, arranging them in one layer on wax paper.

Heat about 1 inch oil in a 4-5-quart heavy pot (preferably cast-iron) until thermometer registers 340 degrees. Working in batches of 4, gently drop patties into hot oil, then fry, turning occasionally, until golden brown, 2-3 minutes, and transfer to paper towels to drain. Return oil to 340 degrees between batches. Serve falafel warm or at room temperature.

Serve with tzatziki sauce, feta cheese, and a salad of mixed shaved vegetables dressed with extra virgin olive oil, lemon juice, salt, and pepper.

WADE SPEES

'Bama Salmon Sandwich

Sourdough isn't critical to this dish: Roule suggests using your favorite bread to build the sandwich. Even without the sourdough, he adds, "It's packed with layers and layers of flavor. The sweet-and-spicy slaw, tangy barbecue and smoke of the salmon just blend so well."

RECIPE BY Scott Roule

1 cup jalapeno coleslaw
3 tablespoons apple cider dressing

2 slices sourdough bread
¾ cup smoked salmon

3 tablespoons Alabama white sauce

Directions:

Mix the slaw and the apple cider dressing; set aside. Spread the salmon on one slice of bread and cover with white sauce. Close the sandwich with the other slice of bread. Press in a panini machine or oven until filling is heated and bread is crisp. Remove the top slice of bread; apply slaw, and then replace the bread. Cut sandwich in half before serving.

ALABAMA WHITE SAUCE

1 cup mayonnaise
2 tablespoons plus 1 teaspoon water
1 teaspoon coarse ground pepper

1 teaspoon whole grain mustard
½ teaspoon kosher salt
½ teaspoon granulated sugar

1 teaspoon minced garlic
1 teaspoon horseradish

Directions:

Mix all ingredients in a bowl until smooth and sugar and salt are dissolved.

JALAPENO COLESLAW

1 cup red cabbage, shaved
½ cup carrot, shredded

½ cup scallion, sliced

¼ cup jalapeno, julienned with seeds

Directions:

Mix all in a bowl.

APPLE CIDER DRESSING

1 cup apple cider vinegar

½ cup granulated sugar

Directions:

In a small saucepan, mix the ingredients together. Simmer until sugar is dissolved: Do not reduce. Refrigerate.

WADE SPEES

SMOKED SALMON

1 lemon
1 cup kosher salt
½ cup brown sugar
1 tablespoon tarragon, chopped

1 tablespoon parsley, chopped
1 tablespoon thyme, chopped
1 bay leaf, crushed
½ teaspoon coriander seeds

1 pound salmon
1 cup cherrywood chips, soaked

Directions:

Slice two wheels from the lemon. Place in a large bowl with remainder of dry ingredients (salt through coriander seeds); mix with hands until well-combined.

Cover the bottom of a deep dish with half of the cure; lay the salmon atop it. Evenly spread remaining cure on top of the salmon, and wrap with plastic. Refrigerate for up to 24 hours.

Remove the salmon from the cure; rinse well and pat dry. Fire the grill. Place the soaked wood chips in a smoking box or aluminum pan. Place the box or pan on the grill and heat until it smolders. Once you have a good smoke, place the salmon on the grill and cover, adjusting the temperature to allow the salmon to absorb as much smoke as possible before cooking all the way through. Remove from heat. Flake the salmon after it's cooled.

French Quarter

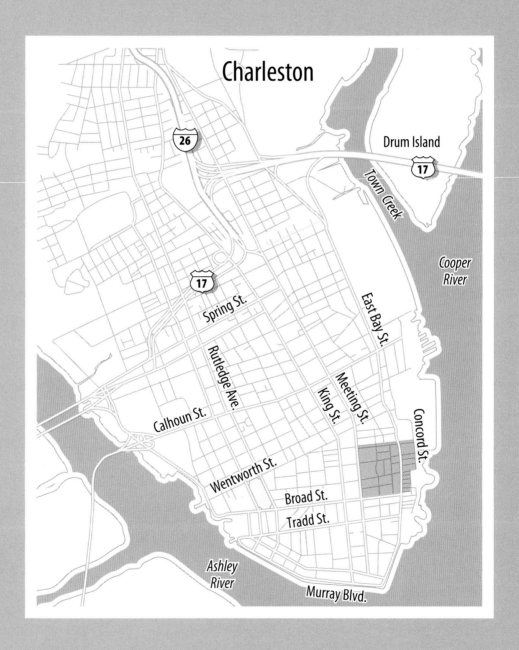

Benne Salsa

No matter what you order at Minero, it's crucial to order the benne salsa. The peanut buttery dip, flecked with chiles, inspired University of South Carolina professor David Shields to tell *Food Republic* that Brock "was the first chef to realize (benne's) central place in the play of flavors that make up the food of our region."

Although benne is kin to modern sesame seeds, they're not interchangeable. The easiest way to buy benne is through ansonmills.com.

RECIPE BY Sean Brock

3½ cups oil	1 teaspoon Mexican oregano	¼ cup salt
½ cup morita chile	½ teaspoon allspice, toasted and	¾ cup apple cider vinegar
¼ cup arbol chile	ground	1½ cups sorghum
¾ cup garlic cloves, crushed	½ teaspoon cumin, toasted and	
4 cups yellow onion, medium dice	ground	
2¼ cups benne seeds		

DIRECTIONS:

Heat oil in a pot, and then deep-fry chiles until aromatic and puffy. When chiles are crunchy, pull them from the oil. Split the oil between two large frying pans. To one of the pans, add garlic and onion; fry until tender and dark around the edges. To the other pan, add benne and fry until light brown. Remove pan from heat and add spices. Blend together chiles, garlic and onions and benne mixture in food processer until a chunky paste forms. Add 1 cup of water and pulse until smooth. Add salt, vinegar and sorghum, and pulse until smooth.

PAUL ZOELLER

Grilled Eggplant with Peperonata, Pesto and Burrata

n Moore's view, summer's most essential tools are eggplant, basil and a grill. "This is a great light appetizer featuring a lot of the local produce available in Charleston," he promises.

RECIPE BY Russ Moore

1 eggplant, sliced into eight skin-on slices
¼ cup blended oil (canola/olive) for grilling eggplant

Salt and pepper
1 cup basil pesto
2 cups peperonata

8-two-ounce balls of burrata, or fresh mozzarella

Directions:

Prepare peperonata and pesto ahead of time. Brush eggplant with blended oil and season with salt and pepper. Grill over hot flame until just tender. Rebrush with blended oil if the eggplant looks like its drying out on the grill. Smear pesto on plate. Lay eggplant slices on pesto, and then top eggplant with peperonata and burrata. Season the burrata with salt and pepper.

PEPERONATA

⅓ cup olive oil
3 red bell peppers, julienned
3 yellow bell peppers, julienned
2 onions, sliced

1 tablespoon garlic
1 cup sherry vinaigrette
¼ cup raw sugar

1 tablespoon capers
½ bunch parsley, chopped
Salt and pepper

Directions:

Heat olive oil in saucepan over medium heat. Sweat bell peppers, onion and garlic until tender. Add sherry vinaigrette and sugar; reduce until vegetables are coated. Stir in capers. Remove from heat and chill. When cool, stir in parsley. Season with salt and pepper.

GRACE BEAHM ALFORD

BASIL PESTO

2 cups basil leaves
2 garlic cloves
¼ cup pine nuts

½ cup olive oil
½ cup Parmesan cheese, grated

Directions:

Combine basil, garlic and pine nuts in food processor. Add oil and process until absorbed. Stir cheese into mixture. Chill.

Crab Rice

Brock is a devoted fan of crab rice, a Lowcountry specialty that's locally associated with Hannibal's Kitchen. Brock's version is a slightly more elaborate affair, made with name-brand ingredients such as Benton's bacon and Anson Mills rice.

This recipe calls for crab roe or mullet bottarga, a favorite ingredient of Brock's that he's likened to country ham. It's harder to find at the grocery store, though: If you're aiming to complete the dish as described, there are a number of online suppliers. Expect to pay about $10 an ounce for the delicacy.

RECIPE BY Sean Brock

¼ cup small diced bacon, preferably Benton's bacon
⅓ cup dried shrimp
1¼ cups very finely diced sweet onion
1 cup very finely diced celery
1 cup very finely diced red bell pepper
2 teaspoons minced garlic

2 tablespoons kosher salt, divided
4 cups water
¼ teaspoon freshly ground white pepper
1 fresh bay leaf
1¼ cups Anson Mills Carolina Gold Rice
7 tablespoons unsalted butter, divided

1 pound lump blue crab meat, picked over for shells and cartilage
1 tablespoon fresh lemon juice
2 tablespoons finely chopped chives
2 tablespoons grated crab roe bottarga (mullet bottarga works as a substitute)

DIRECTIONS:

Put the bacon in a large skillet and cook over medium heat until the bacon starts to soften and the fat renders, about 1 minute. Add the dried shrimp and stir for 1 minute. Add the onion, celery, bell pepper, garlic and 1 tablespoon of kosher salt. Cook, stirring occasionally, until the vegetables are softened, about 6 minutes. Remove from the stove and set aside.

Combine the water, 1 tablespoon of kosher salt, pepper and bay leaf in a medium saucepan. Bring to a boil over medium-high heat, and stir to be sure the salt has dissolved completely. Reduce the heat to medium; add the rice; stir once and bring to a simmer. Simmer gently, uncovered, stirring occasionally, until the rice is al dente, about 10 minutes. Drain. Transfer to a clean medium saucepan. Dice 4 tablespoons of butter and stir into rice. Remove from the stove and cover to keep warm.

Heat 3 tablespoons of butter until foamy in a large skillet over high heat. Add the bacon-and-shrimp mixture and crab. Cook gently without stirring, until the butter begins to brown and the crab is hot and crispy, about 4 minutes. Lightly fold in the lemon juice. Divide the rice among six plates and sprinkle it with chives, evenly divided. Spoon the cooked crab on top; finish by sprinkling with bottarga. Remove bay leaf before serving.

Bittered Holland Sling

A bar called The Gin Joint ought to have Holland-style gin on hand. But years ago, the juniper-forward spirit wasn't easily sourced in South Carolina, so co-owner Joe Raya came up with this recipe to mimic its flavors.

Although the Rayas have specified their favorite brands for this bittered Holland sling, feel free to make reasonable substitutions as needed; the rum listed here, for example, retails for about $50, which makes for a costly one-half ounce garnish if you don't already own a bottle.

RECIPE BY Joe and MariElena Raya

1 ounce gin
1 ounce Redbreast Irish whiskey
¼ ounce Demerara simple syrup

4 dashes Fee Brothers Old Fashioned
  Aromatic Bitters
½ ounce Zacapa 23 rum

Directions:

Combine all ingredients in an ice-filled glass. Top with a float of rum.

DEMERARA SIMPLE SYRUP

½ cup Demerara sugar
½ cup water

Directions:

Combine sugar and water in a saucepan over medium heat, stirring constantly until sugar is dissolved. Cool to room temperature; pour into a glass jar or other airtight container. Simple syrup will keep in the refrigerator for one week.

MICHAEL PRONZATO

Rice Pie with Duck and Oysters

Although this project was designed to produce a snapshot of contemporary Charleston dining, it wouldn't be a complete picture without acknowledging how frequently local chefs probe the past: Parker found his inspiration in *The Centennial Cookbook*, attributed to 'A Southern Lady' and published in 1876.

"We substitute ducks for chicken," Parker says of the changes he's made to the original recipe. "The disc of rice, though certainly not an authentic execution, is equally inspired by Lowcountry culinary tradition, Spanish paella crust, and the crispy, chewy rice crust formed in Korean stone bowl bi bim bop."

RECIPE BY Forrest Parker

6 boneless duck breasts (cleaned, scored and seasoned liberally with kosher salt and pepper)
3 shallots, peeled and julienned
½ cup Madeira
2 tablespoons chopped fresh thyme

2 cups reduced brown stock (duck or chicken)
1 bay leaf
½ stick unsalted butter
1 quart cooked rice (Carolina Gold or Nostrale preferred)

Cooking oil
4 tablespoons benne seeds
24 shucked oysters
Butter
Salt and pepper

DIRECTIONS:

Heat a heavy skillet, such as cast iron, on low heat. Place duck breasts skin side down and allow to render slowly. When skin is crispy, turn breasts and allow them to continue cooking another 3-4 minutes; this will produce a medium doneness. Remove from heat and allow to rest before slicing.

In a medium sauce pan over medium heat, lightly caramelize the shallots. Deglaze pan with Madeira, burning off the alcohol and reducing by two-thirds. Add stock, thyme, bay leaf and reduce by half, or to a slightly thickened consistency. Whisk in butter and remove from heat.

Preheat oven to 350 degrees.

Heat a nonstick skillet or well-greased cast-iron skillet over medium-high heat. Add enough cooking oil (or rendered duck fat) to thinly coat the skillet, followed by ½ cup of cooked rice. Using a spatula and working quickly, mash the rice into a flat disc and continue cooking. Add a generous pinch of benne seed and season with salt and pepper. If using medium- or long-grain rice, add a dash of water to release additional rice starch. When a golden crust forms, remove from heat and repeat procedure for 6 crusts.

Arrange the crusts on a sheet tray and put them in the oven. Return sauce to a simmer and add shucked oysters. Cook for about a minute, or until edges just begin to ruffle, and remove from heat.

Slice duck breasts on the bias and plate. Spoon oyster sauce over duck, remove bay leaf before serving. Remove warmed rice discs from oven; put one on each plate. Pair with a sauteed seasonal green.

GRACE BEAHM ALFORD

As printed in *The Centennial Cookbook*, 1876

Boil a pint of rice rather soft, but not gluey, also boil a pair of chickens. While the rice is warm stir into it a large spoonful of butter, season with black pepper, a teaspoon of made mustard and a little salt; then add three eggs well beaten. Put half of the rice in a baking dish, cut up the chickens and lay on it; then cover them with the rest, and bake.

Fall in Florida Fruit Salad

When it's spring in Charleston, Lira conjures fall in Florida with this fruit salad that tastes as bright as it looks. While you can pickle the beets and grind the peppercorns at home, it's fine to buy pickled beets and ground Sichuan pepper before embarking on your virtual Florida trip. And if there's no chicory at the market, radicchio work, too.

RECIPE BY Alex Lira

6 blood oranges	Olive oil (to taste)	1 quart chicory
2 sweet grapefruits	1 cup hazelnuts	1 cup mint leaves
20 kumquats	1 tablespoon Sichuan peppercorn	20 leaves of tarragon
1 cup pickled beets, liquid reserved	Salt	

DIRECTIONS:

Preheat oven to 275 degrees.

Segment blood orange and grapefruit with a very sharp knife, working over a container so none of the juice is lost.

Place segments in a second container. Halve kumquats and add to container holding blood orange and grapefruit segments.

Place pickled beets and citrus juice in a blender or Vitamix. Blend until everything spins. If there's not enough liquid to pick up the beets, add reserved pickling juice until they're unstuck.

Add olive oil to beet puree slowly, blending until velvety and not too thick; aim for a vinaigrette consistency. Season to taste.

Spread shelled hazelnuts over a baking pan. Roast for about 10-15 minutes, or until skins brown.

While hazelnuts are roasting, heat peppercorns in a frying pan over medium-heat. When peppercorns become fragrant and darken, remove them from heat. Cool and grind using a spice grinder or mortar and pestle; alternatively, crush the peppercorns with a heavy rolling pin.

Scatter ground peppercorns over roasted hazelnuts. Salt liberally. Rough chop nuts.

Add chicory and mint to bowl of citrus segments. Pour beet puree over salad until it's just lightly coated. Gently mix, taste and make any necessary adjustments. Divide among six plates. Garnish with tarragon and hazelnut mixture.

Ansonborough

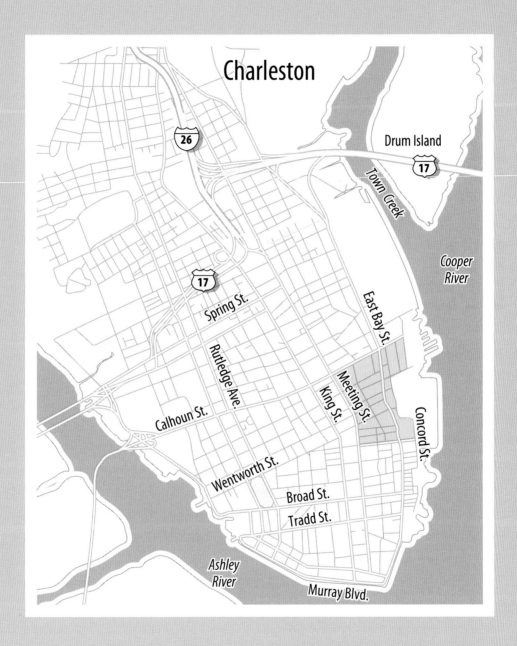

Roasted Cauliflower Steaks

This recipe yields two trendy ingredients: Cauliflower steaks, or cauliflower sliced lengthwise, and cauliflower "rice," which are tiny bits of the white vegetables. But FIG owner Mike Lata developed this preparation before either item was much in vogue.

"This is the kind of dish that garnered tons of fans in FIG's early days," he says. "At one point we sold so much cauliflower that it became one cook's full time job to prepare it."

The cauliflower was so popular that even though it hasn't appeared on the menu for years, customers still ask for the recipe.

RECIPE BY Mike Lata

2 tablespoons water, plus more as needed
2 tablespoons whole-grain mustard
2 tablespoons Dijon mustard
½ pound (2 sticks) cold butter, cubed
1 lemon, juiced

Coarse kosher salt, to taste
2 tablespoons canola oil
1 head cauliflower, cut lengthwise into 1-inch "steaks"
Capers, to garnish
Parsley leaves, to garnish

Celery heart leaves, to garnish
Toasted breadcrumbs, to garnish
Radish, thinly sliced, to garnish
Sea salt and freshly ground pepper, to taste

DIRECTIONS:

Preheat oven to 350 degrees.

Combine water and mustards in a small heavy-bottomed saucepan and bring to a simmer. Reduce heat to medium and quickly whisk in the cubes of butter, one or two at a time, until creamy and emulsified. Remove from heat and season with lemon juice and salt. If you have an immersion blender, you can blend the sauce to help stabilize the emulsion.

Have some warm water on hand to lighten up the mixture, as it tends to thicken. Keep sauce warm while you prepare the cauliflower.

Turn head of cauliflower upside down. Cut off the rounded edges to the right and left of the stem and reserve for another use (you can make cauliflower "rice" with these scraps). You are now left with the center of the cauliflower.

Cut lengthwise into even "steaks" about 1-inch thick. A large head should yield 2 or 3 pieces.

Coat the bottom of a 9-inch iron skillet or nonstick saute pan with canola oil, season with 1 teaspoon salt, and set over medium heat. Add cauliflower to the pan one piece at a time and cook until sizzling and golden brown. Turn onto a sheet pan lined with aluminum foil and repeat until all the steaks are browned. Roast in a preheated oven for 10-15 minutes, just until tender enough to pierce with a fork.

Arrange cauliflower seared-side-up on a warm platter and drizzle with the warm mustard butter. Garnish with capers, parsley, celery leaves, toasted breadcrumbs and thinly sliced radish. Season with coarse sea salt and a few turns of freshly cracked black pepper.

GRACE BEAHM ALFORD

Pressurized Octopus

T his is an equipment-heavy recipe, calling for a grill fired by two different fuels, as well as a pressure cooker. But the technique is fairly straightforward: Instacure is a salt and sodium nitrate blend that can be ordered online from sources such as Amazon or ChefSteps.

RECIPE BY Vinson Petrillo

½ cup olive oil	6 garlic cloves, peeled	½ cup white wine
1 fennel bulb	Salt	Red chili flakes
1 large onion	1¼ cups red wine vinegar	1 octopus, 5-6 pounds

Directions:

Put the olive oil in a pressure cooker and turn heat to medium. Roughly cut fennel, onion and garlic; add to pressure cooker. Sprinkle a pinch of salt over the vegetables and oil. Let vegetables sweat for 3 minutes. Add the red wine vinegar, wine and chili flakes; bring to a boil. Add octopus. Secure the lid and set to full pressure. Once pressure reaches 15 psi, cook the octopus for exactly 17 minutes. Release pressure and portion octopus into 3-ounce pieces. Allow octopus to come to room temperature, and then char pieces on a hot wood-burning grill before serving.

LAMB BELLY

2 lamb breasts	2 tablespoons sugar	⅛ teaspoon coriander seed
½ teaspoon Instacure #2	⅛ teaspoon toasted fennel seed	1 tablespoon black peppercorns
3½ tablespoons salt	⅛ teaspoon red chili flakes	1 quart rendered lamb fat or duck fat

Directions:

Mix all dry ingredients together and spread over all sides of the lamb breasts. Place in a nonreactive container and cover for 24 hours.

Preheat oven to 310 degrees. Remove lamb from container and rinse off the cure. Dry with a towel and place in a Dutch oven covered completely with the lamb fat. Put on the stove and heat to 212 degrees. Once it reaches temperature, place covered lamb in the oven for 3 hours or until fork-tender. Remove lamb from the fat and press between two sheet trays. Put a weight on the top tray, and refrigerate lamb overnight. Remove from refrigerator and cut into 1½-inch diamonds. Reserve.

HERBED MARCONA ALMOND CONDIMENT

1 cup toasted Marcona almonds	2 bunches parsley leaves	1 clove garlic	Juice from 1 lemon
	2 bunches cilantro leaves	½ cup olive oil	Salt and pepper

GRACE BEAHM ALFORD

Directions:

Place all ingredients in a food processor and process until incorporated. Taste and adjust seasoning accordingly.

EGGPLANT

2 large eggplants	Salt and pepper	1 clove garlic
¼ cup olive oil	1 preserved lemon, skin only	4 tablespoons fresh lemon juice

Directions:

Preheat oven to 450 degrees. Slice the eggplant in two, and season halves with about half of the olive oil, and salt and pepper. Place cut side down on a nonstick silicone baking liner or parchment paper. Roast in the oven for 30 minutes, or until very tender.

Cool for 10 minutes before handling; use a spoon to scrape out the inside of the eggplant. Place the flesh in a food processor with salt, pepper, preserved lemon skin, garlic and lemon juice. Mix on high for 2 minutes and slowly emulsify the remaining olive oil into the mix. Taste and season; reserve in a lidded container.

ASSEMBLY

Olive oil	Garlic, sliced	Barrel-aged soy sauce Herbs

Directions:

Grill octopus on a very hot charcoal grill, until it begins to char on the tips. Once hot, allow octopus to rest in a small bath of olive oil and sliced garlic.

Place the lamb on the coolest part of the grill and allow to render and crisp for about 5-6 minutes. Brush with a barrel-aged soy sauce and keep hot.

Shape the eggplant into a quenelle on a plate, and then quenelle the herb condiment alongside. Place 1 piece of octopus in the center of the plate, 1 piece of lamb near the eggplant and 1 piece of lamb near the condiment. Garnish with small herb leaves and serve.

Poke

Prior to 2016, Hawaii's favorite way of preparing raw fish was hardly known on the mainland. Now the words "ahi poke for two" have a romantic ring to them. To really impress your significant other, follow Sandole's advice and buy the best sushi-grade tuna available; to earn a No. 1 rating, tuna must be fresh, fat, smooth and shiny.

RECIPE BY Jesse Sandole

10 ounces sushi grade
    No. 1 yellowfin tuna
¼ cup soy caramel
3 teaspoons lime juice

1 tablespoon sriracha
10-15 large cilantro leaves
1 tablespoon sesame seeds

DIRECTIONS:

Combine ingredients in a tall pot and place over medium heat. Whisk ingredients together and bring mixture to a simmer. Stir occasionally until mixture is reduced by one-third. Remove from heat and allow to cool.

WADE SPEES

Tomato Caramel, Bacon Jam and Goat Cheese Hamburger

t's hard to have a full discussion of burgers in the 2010s without referencing bacon jam, which also graced the popular patty at Artisan Meat Share. This is Zucker's favorite way to make and showcase the red-meat condiment.

RECIPE BY John Zucker

2 pounds ground Angus beef	8 ounces goat cheese (or cheese of	½ cup smoked tomato caramel
Salt and pepper	your choice)	Lettuce, tomato and onions, for
4 hamburger buns	½ cup bacon jam	garnish

Directions:

Heat a saute pan over medium-low heat.

Divide ground beef into four 8-ounce patties. Pat each burger into a round flat shape. Make a dimple in the center of the meat. Season both sides of the burger liberally with salt and pepper.

Add burgers to pan, turning heat up to medium. Cook until meat forms a crust on the side that is cooking, then flip the patty. Continue to cook until the second side has formed a crust. Flip once again. Place goat cheese on the burger and cook for 2 minutes. Remove from heat and let rest for a few minutes.

Place each cheeseburger on bottom half of a bun. Put about 2 tablespoons of bacon jam on top of the cheese. Pour about 2 tablespoons of smoked tomato caramel atop jam. Garnish with lettuce, tomato and onions, if desired.

SMOKED TOMATO CARAMEL

8 large vine-ripened tomatoes	4 cups sugar

Directions:

Smoke tomatoes in a smoker for two hours. After removing tomatoes, push them through a ricer, reserving liquid in a small bowl. Squeeze all of the liquid from the tomato pulp into the bowl. Strain the liquid through a fine chinois to remove any tomato pulp. Put liquid in a 4-quart saucepan. Add the sugar and mix well. Bring the mixture to a boil and then reduce heat to simmer. Cook until the sauce thickens and turns the color of dark burgundy, approximately 1 hour. Remove from heat. Let cool at room temperature. Do not refrigerate.

CHRIS HANCLOSKY

BACON JAM

8 cups bacon, uncooked and chopped
1 red onion, diced

2 to 3 vine-ripened tomatoes, roughly chopped
1 cup apple cider vinegar

1½ cups brown sugar

Directions:

Put bacon in a 10-quart braiser or rondeau pan over medium heat. Cook slowly until the bacon is almost fully cooked and all of the fat is rendered.

Add the red onion and saute until the onions are darker or caramelized. Add the tomato. Continue to cook until the tomatoes break down.

Add the vinegar and reduce by half. Add the brown sugar and mix well. Cook at a simmer and continue to reduce until thick. Take the mixture off the heat and cool for 20 minutes.

Put the mixture in a food processor a few tablespoons at a time. Pulse the mixture twice and repeat with the rest of the mixture. The jam should still be a little chunky.

Radcliffeborough

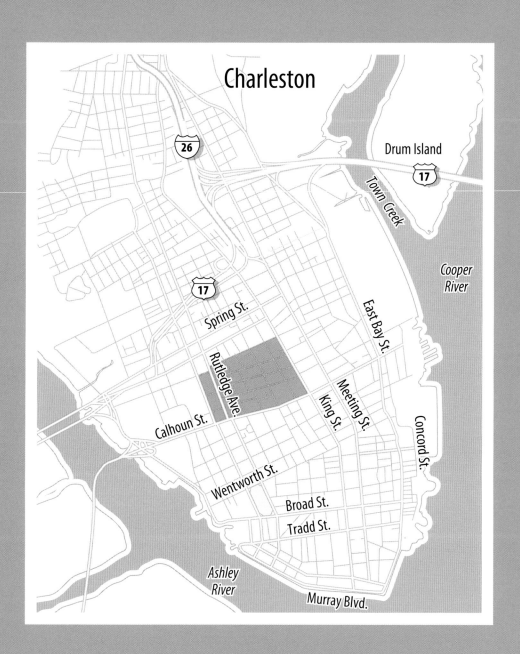

Charleston

Pho Ga

Phi frames his warning in the gentlest of terms: "Pho is definitely a labor of love." In other words, it's not a soup you throw together for a quick weeknight meal. But the Pink Bellies owner insists the investment is worthwhile.

"The aromas draw the family into the kitchen," he promises.

For home cooks pressed for time, premade chicken stock is the most obvious shortcut. But "the flavors will be off," Phi says. "Store-bought stocks contain other flavorings such as celery and carrots, and sodium will have to be adjusted."

RECIPE BY Thai Phi

4 large knobs of ginger	10 star anise pods	White onion, thinly sliced
1 large onion	1 small bark of Saigon cinnamon	Bean sprouts
2 (3-pound) chickens, boned	12 coriander seeds	Thai basil
1 sliced large knob of ginger	5 cloves	Lime
3 tablespoons fish sauce	Fresh rice noodles	Hoisin sauce
¼ cup kosher salt, plus more to taste	Spring onions, chopped	Sriracha sauce
1 cup rock sugar	Cilantro, chopped	

DIRECTIONS:

Peel ginger and quarter the onion. Roast at 300 degrees for 1 hour to intensify flavors. Cool ginger and slice.

Bone chickens and remove skin except from chicken breast. Add chicken bones, chicken skin to 12-quart pot; fill with water. Add kosher salt. Boil for 45 seconds to 1 minute. Drain, reserving skin and bones. Rinse bones of impurities. Rinse pot of impurities or use a new pot.

Return bones to pot and fill with water, leaving 3 inches at the top. Simmer. Never let the broth come to a hard boil as it will turn cloudy and become flat. Simmer for 2 hours.

While the broth simmers, marinate chicken meat in 3 tablespoons of fish sauce and 1 large knob of sliced ginger. Roast until internal temperature reaches 165 degrees. When chickens cool, shred or pull dark meat; slice the breasts with skin on.

To the broth pot, add sliced roasted ginger and onion. Season with kosher salt and rock sugar until desired saltiness and sweetness is almost reached. Flavors will continue to concentrate as the broth simmers for another hour.

Toast spices (anise pods through cloves) in a skillet until spices are barely charred and aromas deepen. Arrange spices atop cheesecloth, tie into a bag and steep in broth. Simmer the broth for another hour.

Taste broth and season accordingly to your taste buds. Remove broth from heat.

Soak noodles in cold water until they are ready to be cooked. Bring a pot of water to a boil. Using a noodle strainer, dip noodles into boiling water for 10-20 seconds and continue to swirl with chopsticks until al dente. Strain well and place into bowl.

Add chopped spring onions, sliced white onions and chopped cilantro to the middle of the bowl. Surround with cooked chicken

GRACE BEAHM ALFORD

meat. Pour hot broth over meat. Enjoy the labor of your hard-earned broth before adjusting with Thai basil and lime. Dip meat into hoisin or sriracha sauces. Add bean sprouts for additional texture. Adjust broth with Thai basil and fresh lime juice.

Spicy Shrimp Salad

When I reviewed The Darling, I wrote, "It's easy to imagine a home cook being the envy of her bridge club after serving up The Darling's shrimp salad, a cream cheese concoction prickled with chili paste and pickled red onions." It's a phrase I forgot until chef DiMaio reminded me of it. When asked to supply a recipe for the cookbook, he wisely suggested this salad. Bridge club members, prepare to be wowed.

RECIPE BY Joe DiMaio

1 cup diced red onion
Red wine vinegar
1 pound shrimp

16 ounces whipped cream cheese
1 ounce chili paste or sriracha
½ cup scallion

Salt and pepper

Directions:

Add diced red onion to a bowl with enough red wine vinegar to cover. Soak for 2 hours; then discard vinegar.

Fill a pot with salted water and boil. Peel and devein shrimp; poach shrimp in salted water. Shock in ice bath and set aside.

Rough cut cooked shrimp and combine with pickled red onions, cream cheese, chili paste and scallions. Fold together with a rubber spatula, season with salt and pepper.

WHEAT THINS

6 ounces whole-wheat flour
1 tablespoon sugar
2 teaspoons salt

2 tablespoons butter, room
    temperature
2 tablespoons water, cold

Directions:

Preheat oven to 350 degrees. Combine all ingredients, except for water, in a food processor. Pulse a few times until butter is pea size. Once this happens, turn on food processor, and slowly drizzle water into the dough until a ball forms. Put ball on well-floured surface, and roll out dough until as thin as possible. Cut dough into 1½-inch squares; put them on a parchment-lined sheet tray. Make small holes in each square with the tines of a fork. Sprinkle salt on crackers before placing them into the oven.

Bake crackers for 12 minutes. Allow them to cool before storing.

GRACE BEAHM ALFORD

Bourbon-Glazed Pork Shoulder

There are no guarantees during football season: Maybe your team will win, maybe it won't. But if you start up a pork shoulder one day before kickoff, you're at least promised a satisfying meal. Bacon likes to pair the glazed meat with butterbeans (cooked down with more pork, of course).

RECIPE BY Jeremiah Bacon

Pork shoulder (10-15 pounds)	Pepper	Sorghum bacon glaze
Salt	Pork fat	

Directions:

Preheat oven to 300 degrees.

Season pork shoulder liberally with salt and pepper. Place in a Dutch oven or other deep pan. Cover with pork fat and cover pan with lid or foil. Cook for 10-12 hours.

Remove from oven and let cool completely. Gently remove any bones from the shoulder and transfer pork shoulder to a different pan. Reserve pork fat. Place another pan on top of the pork shoulder. Top with a few cans or other heavy items to press; refrigerate for 12-24 hours.

Preheat oven to 300 degrees. Slice pork. Reheat slices in a medium-high oven-proof saute pan with a small amount of oil. Sear each slice on one side, and then return pork to pan. Bake for about 8 minutes. Remove pork from oven and top with sorghum bacon glaze.

SORGHUM BACON GLAZE

1 yellow onion, medium dice	¼ pound smoked bacon	1 gallon pork stock or mixture of
1 carrot, medium dice	3 cups port wine	stock and chicken broth
2 ribs celery, medium dice	3 cups red wine	Salt
1 bay leaf	1 cup sorghum molasses	Pepper
1 star anise	¼ cup bourbon	

Directions:

Sweat onion, carrot, celery, bay leaf, star anise and bacon until vegetables are lightly caramelized. Add port wine and red wine; cook until nearly all of the liquid is dissolved. Add ½ of the sorghum molasses and cook until slightly thickened. Add pork stock and bourbon. Bring entire mixture to a boil. Once boiling, reduce to a simmer and let entire mixture reduce by one-quarter to one-half. Season with salt, pepper and remaining sorghum. Strain and cool. Remove bay leaf before serving.

WADE SPEES

Gin & Tonic

Who needs a recipe for gin and tonic? Charleston's cocktail scene, as it turned out. This now-famous Proof cocktail so impressed William Grant ambassador Charlotte Voisey that she started talking up the bar (and the city's drinking culture generally) to international audiences.

"It is the drink that kind of put us on the map, if you will," Nelson says. "It's a great combination of sweet and tart, refreshing and appropriate for most months of the year here in Charleston."

RECIPE BY Craig Nelson

1½ ounces Hendrick's Gin	1 dash Bitter Truth lemon bitters	1 strip of orange peel
½ ounce freshly squeezed lemon juice	2 quarter-inch slices of cucumber	Seagram's Tonic Water
	1 strip of lemon peel	Collins glass

DIRECTIONS:

Combine gin, lemon juice, bitters and 1 slice of cucumber in a shaker with ice and shake vigorously. Strain into Collins glass; repeat the process so all cucumber pieces are removed.

Fill glass with ice. Twist the lemon and orange peels above the glass and then drop them into the gin mixture.

Fill glass with tonic and stir quickly. Garnish with the remaining slice of cucumber.

WADE SPEES

Westside

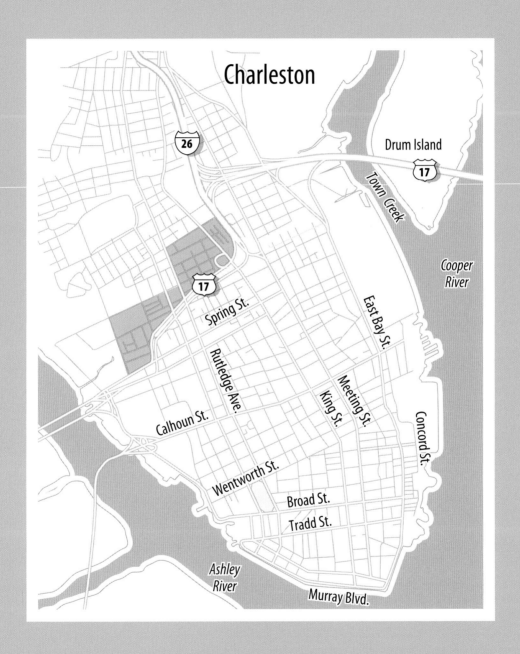

Black-Eyed Pea Salad

Leon's is possibly best known for chargrilled oysters, polished with cheese, and fried chicken with crisp skin. Yet the Upper King Street restaurant stealthily serves lots of fresh vegetables, such as the peppers and cucumbers called for by this black-eyed pea preparation. "This dish exemplifies the lightness that is consistent throughout our menu, an attempt to update the Southern larder," co-owner Brooks Reitz says.

RECIPE BY Leon's Oyster Shop

1 cup dried black-eyed peas
4 ⅔ cups onions, medium dice
2 ⅓ cups celery, medium dice
1 tablespoon salt

⅔ cup olive oil
2 ⅓ cups red peppers, medium dice
2 ⅓ cups green peppers, medium dice

1½ cups white wine vinegar
2 ⅓ cups cucumbers, quartered and cut into ½-inch pieces
Fresh chives

DIRECTIONS:

Soak dried black-eyed peas overnight, then cook in salted water until tender. If possible, let cool in the cooking liquid to retain salinity. Sweat onions and celery in a medium-sized pan with salt and olive oil until creamy. Add peppers and cook until tender. Add vinegar and cucumbers and remove from heat.

Add ⅓ cup of the vegetable relish to 2 cups of black-eyed peas; add olive oil and salt to taste. Garnish with fresh chives.

WADE SPEES

Blistered Shishito Peppers in Vanilla Vinaigrette

LEIGH-ANN BEVERLEY

Vegetables are everywhere at Harold's Cabin, including on the second-floor back deck, where the restaurant cultivates them. But the undisputed star of the forage board, which chef Justin Pfau designed to ape a charcuterie plate, is the shishito pepper. Pfau calls this preparation "simple, straightforward and semi-rustic."

RECIPE BY Justin Pfau

12 shishito peppers	½ cup Champagne vinaigrette	1 cup Romesco sauce
1 tablespoon olive oil	Sea salt	Toasted pistachios for garnish (See Cook's Note)

Directions:

Clean and stem peppers. Heat olive oil in a saute pan over medium heat until warm. Add peppers to pan; toss and turn them frequently.

Cook for approximately 5-7 minutes.

Remove peppers from pan and toss in bowl with Champagne vinaigrette. Salt to taste. To serve, lay peppers on a plate and sauce with Romesco. Grate pistachios over sauce.

CHAMPAGNE VINAIGRETTE

1 vanilla pod	4 tablespoons Champagne vinegar
¾ cup olive oil	Sea salt

Directions:

Split the vanilla pod and scrape seeds into a bowl. Add oil and vinegar; whisk until combined. Salt to taste.

ROMESCO SAUCE

2 red bell peppers	¼ cup olive oil	¼ teaspoon cayenne pepper
½ cup toasted pistachios	2 tablespoons sherry vinegar	Sea salt
½ cup bread crumbs	¼ teaspoon paprika	

WADE SPEES

Directions:

Preheat oven to 500 degrees. Place peppers on cookie sheet and cook for 30-40 minutes, or until their skins wrinkle fully and char. Remove stems and seeds. Blend in food processor with remaining ingredients, pistachios through cayenne pepper. Salt to taste.

COOK'S NOTE

Toast pistachios by spreading the nuts on a cookie sheet; cook in a 350-degree oven for 5 min.

Crudite with Avocado Mousse

There was a time when American restaurants that made a big deal about their beef would offer a stuffed tomato or hamburger patty with iceberg lettuce, dishes generally listed to keep "lady customers" happy.

Nowadays, most steakhouse owners have gotten wise to the fact that vegetable interest knows no gender bounds; fresh produce regularly appears all over the meatiest of menus. No local restaurant better exemplifies that trend than Little Jack's Tavern.

RECIPE BY John Amato

CRUDITE

Assortment of seasonal vegetables, such as asparagus, baby carrots, English cucumber, radishes, okra

Extra-virgin olive oil
Fleur de sel
Chives

Directions:

Peel and slice vegetables into shapes conducive for dipping; smaller vegetables may be left whole or halved. Finely slice chives into small rounds for garnishing.

Arrange vegetables in a bowl. Drizzle with olive oil; sprinkle with fleur de sel and chives. Serve with avocado mousse.

AVOCADO MOUSSE

1 medium ripe Hass avocado, peeled and pitted
3 tablespoons chives or green onion, chopped

3 tablespoons tarragon, chopped
1 clove of garlic, minced
½ cup heavy cream
1 egg yolk

1 tablespoon lemon juice
1 teaspoon salt
½ cup extra virgin olive oil

Directions:

Place all ingredients into a high-powered blender and blend at high speed for 2 minutes or until the ingredients are fully incorporated and the mousse is silky smooth. Chill mousse in the refrigerator until cold.

WADE SPEES

King Street Historic District

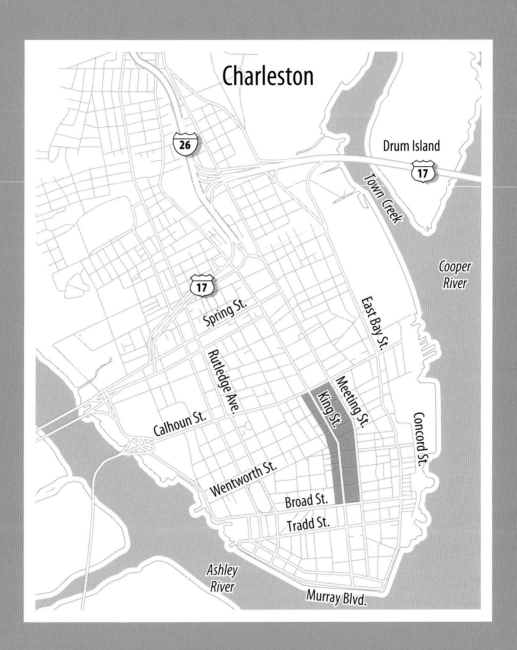

Summer Rolls

This appetizer makes grocery shopping easy, since its ingredient list consists almost solely of single fruits and vegetables. If you end up with extra peanut sauce, toss it with cold rice noodles for an equally simple summer salad.

RECIPE BY Masanori Shiraishi

1 cucumber
1 mango, peeled
1 red bell pepper
1 jalapeno

1 head iceberg lettuce
1 bunch of cilantro, trimmed
1 avocado
1 bunch mint

1 pack large rice wrappers
Peanut sauce

Directions:

Slice cucumber into ¼-inch discs, and then slice each disc into two or three sticks. Slice mango, red pepper, jalapeno and lettuce into equal-size sticks. Quarter the avocado.

Soak rice wrapper in warm water for about 5 seconds. Shake off water, then carefully lay on cutting board, without letting the wrapper fold back on itself. Lay about ¼ of the mint leaves about 2 inches from the bottom of the rice wrapper.

Top with a handful of lettuce, and then cover with about ¼ of the cilantro. Add one slice of avocado, 4-6 pieces of mango, 4-6 pieces of red bell pepper and 3 jalapeno slices. Put a few cucumbers on top.

Bring the bottom of the wrapper over the vegetable pile. Tuck it in tightly; roll once and then pull in both sides of the wrapper. Roll closed. Serve with peanut sauce.

PEANUT SAUCE

16 ounces peanut butter
16 ounces hoisin sauce

¼ cup sugar
3 cups water

Directions:

Pour ingredients into saucepan. Simmer for 5 minutes over medium heat, whisking intermittently.

GRACE BEAHM ALFORD

Crab Cakes

Charleston Grill considers Weaver's crab cake one of its signature dishes. The pear tomatoes used whole in the sauce are an heirloom variety of tomatoes with sloping shoulders. If you can't find them, other bite-size tomatoes named for fruits, such as grape or cherry, are an acceptable substitute.

RECIPE BY Michelle Weaver

1 lemon
½ cup mayonnaise
1 egg white
1 tablespoon chives

1 tablespoon thyme
Salt and ground white pepper
1 pound crab meat

2 tablespoons breadcrumbs, made in food processor from fresh white bread with crusts removed

Directions:

Halve lemon. Zest one half; juice the other half. Add both to a bowl with mayonnaise, egg white, chives and thyme. Salt and pepper the mixture. Fold in the crab meat. Make a patty from about one-sixth of the mixture; dust with bread crumbs and sear in butter or oil in a pan over high heat. Repeat five times. Plate each cake individually and top with sauce.

CRAB CAKE SAUCE

2 shallots, chopped fine
½ cup extra-virgin olive oil

6 peeled shrimp, deveined and cut into julienne strips
10 red pear tomatoes

10 yellow pear tomatoes
2 limes, juiced
2 tablespoons fresh dill

Directions:

Heat shallots in oil, then add shrimp and cook. Add remaining ingredients and heat through.

WADE SPEES

Eastside and
Mazyck-Wraggborough

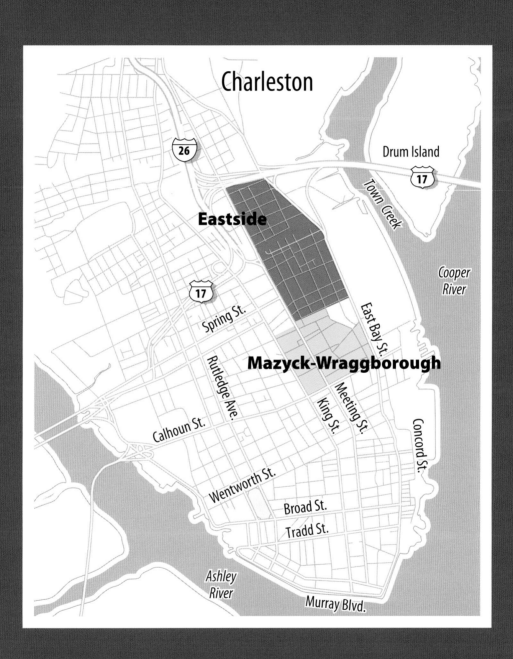

V for Verdita

Verdita is a spirits-friendly green juice from Mexico, where it's shot before tequila or sipped alongside it. Bartenders fond of patriotic origin stories like to point out that completing the lineup with a shot of sangrita (a tomato-based drink) makes for the colors of the Mexican flag. Yet in the U.S., summery verdita is rarely a three-glass proposition: It's typically mixed with tequila.

RECIPE BY Teddy Nixon

1¼ ounces silver tequila	½ ounce fresh lime juice	Smoked salt
¾ ounce chile liqueur, such as Ancho Reyes	½ ounce cucumber simple syrup	Mint sprig
	2 ounces verdita	

Directions:

Put all ingredients in a shaker tin with ice and shake hard. Double-strain over new ice into a Collins glass rimmed with smoked salt. Top with a mint sprig.

CUCUMBER SYRUP

2 cups sugar
2 cups water

1 large English cucumber

Directions:

Combine sugar and water in a pot over medium-high heat; bring to a boil. Using a cheese grater, grate cucumbers into syrup. Once mixture is fully combined, remove from heat. Cover and let sit for at least 30 minutes. Refrigerated in an airtight container, syrup will last about a week.

VERDITA

1 large can pineapple juice (about 46 ounces)	¾ bunch mint, picked	1 large bar spoon of ascorbic acid, to preserve color
1 bunch cilantro	1½ large jalapenos	

Directions:

Combine all ingredients in a Vitamix; blend on high until well incorporated. Double strain through a conical mesh strainer. Verdita will last about five days in a refrigerator.

CHRIS HANCLOSKY

Tomato-Berry Gazpacho

W hen Nate Whiting was stationed at 492, he prided himself on blending ingredients that rarely appear in close proximity. For this soup, he applied that approach to tomatoes and white chocolate. "The unexpected makes the dish memorable," Whiting says.

RECIPE BY Nate Whiting

28 ounces of peeled San Marzano tomatoes
1 pint fresh raspberries
⅓ pint strawberries, hulled
⅓ English cucumber, peeled and chopped

¼ cup roasted red pepper, peeled and seeded.
1 ⅓ tablespoons red onion, minced
1 teaspoon coriander, ground
3 tablespoons extra-virgin olive oil or vanilla oil (recipe follows)
Cold water

Agave syrup or honey, to taste
Kosher salt, to taste
Banyuls or sherry vinegar, to taste
Sea salt, for garnish
Cucumber, for garnish
Cherry tomato, for garnish
Cilantro, for garnish

Directions:

Puree ingredients tomatoes through coriander in a blender until smooth. Pour the gazpacho into a container and whisk oil into it. If needed, thin with cold water.

Season to taste with sweetener, salt and vinegar. Strain the soup if you prefer a smoother consistency. Chill completely before serving. Garnish with white chocolate custard, vanilla oil, sea salt, cucumber, cherry tomato and cilantro.

WHITE CHOCOLATE CUSTARD

½ cup chopped white chocolate, such as Valrhona
¼ cup cold butter, small diced
¼ cup sugar

1½ tablespoons cornstarch
¼ teaspoon kosher salt
2 egg yolks

1 cup whole milk
½ cup heavy cream
¼ vanilla bean

Directions:

In a large bowl, combine the chopped white chocolate with butter; set aside. In a second large bowl, whisk together sugar, cornstarch and salt. Add the egg yolks to the sugar mix and whisk until smooth. Set aside.

Add milk and heavy cream to a large saucepan. Scrape the vanilla bean seeds into the milk and cream and bring to a simmer. Do not boil. Carefully pour and temper the hot cream into the egg yolk mixture while

GRACE BEAHM ALFORD

whisking.

Return the custard to the stove and carefully cook, while whisking until the mixture reaches 180 degrees. Pour the mixture into the bowl of white chocolate and butter; stir until completely melted and smooth. Chill and serve as desired.

VANILLA OIL

½ cup grapeseed or canola oil   1 vanilla bean, split and scraped

Directions:

In a small pot, combine the oil and vanilla. Over medium heat, warm the oil to 180 degrees, while stirring often. Cool the oil. Remove the pod and squeeze out remaining seeds. Refrigerate. The seeds will settle, so be sure to stir or shake before use.

North Central and NOMO (North Morrison)

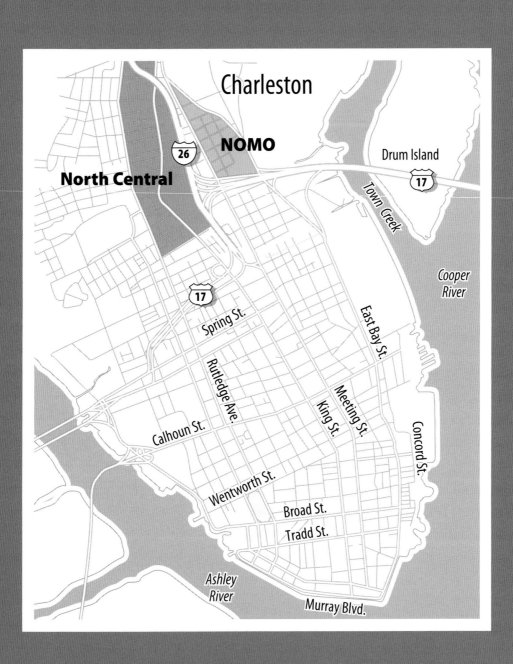

Poached Grouper

M att Canter's poached grouper with tomato-fennel broth has a Mediterranean accent, but it's an ideal recipe for colder days, since it requires standing over three separate simmering pots. You can purchase premade fish stock from a gourmet retail or perhaps a fishmonger.

RECIPE BY Matt Canter

1 gallon court bouillon
6 (5-ounce) portions of grouper, skin and bloodline removed
1 quart tomato-fennel broth

1 pound mussels
4 ounces butter
½ bunch flat-leaf parsley, chopped

3 pounds fingerling potatoes, boiled and skinned
Fennel salad
Olive oil

Directions:

Heat court bouillon (poaching liquid) to 180 degrees. Add fish fillets to the liquid, turning occasionally for about 8 minutes. In a separate saute pan, combine the tomato-fennel broth, mussels, butter, parsley and potatoes. Cook over high heat until the mussels open, about 5 minutes.

Place each poached fillet in the center of a large shallow bowl. Spoon the mussel mixture over and around the fish. Remove bay leaves. Garnish with fennel salad, divided equally between the six bowls. Drizzle with olive oil and serve.

TOMATO-FENNEL BROTH

2 cups white onion, chopped
1 cup celery, chopped
1 leek, chopped
5 garlic cloves, minced
1 cup white wine

2 cups canned whole tomatoes
2 tablespoons tomato paste
1 teaspoon saffron
5 quarts fish stock

6 sprigs of thyme and 6 bay leaves, tied together with twine
Salt, to taste
Hot sauce, to taste

Directions:

Heat a 12-quart saucepot over medium-high heat. Add onion, celery and leek; sweat until very tender. Add the garlic and cook for another 2 minutes. Add the wine and reduce by half.

Add the tomatoes, tomato paste, saffron, fish stock and herbs. Bring to a boil and then simmer, stirring occasionally to avoid sticking, until it has reduced to just over a gallon.

Puree mixture in a blender until very smooth. Pass through a fine-mesh strainer. Season the mixture with salt and hot sauce. Set aside.

WADE SPEES

COURT BOUILLON (POACHING LIQUID)

5 quarts water	2 celery ribs, finely chopped	6 thyme sprigs
1 quart white wine	1 small leek, finely chopped	¼ teaspoon black peppercorns
1 cup white distilled vinegar	1 fennel bulb, finely chopped	
1 medium onion, finely chopped	6-8 parsley stems	

Directions:

Bring all ingredients to a boil and simmer for 30 minutes or until all of the vegetables are soft. Strain through a fine-mesh strainer and set aside. Court bouillon will keep in the refrigerator for about a week.

FENNEL SALAD

1 fennel bulb	Lemon juice, to taste
½ pound jumbo lump crab	Olive oil, to taste
½ bunch flat-leaf parsley	Salt, to taste

Directions:

Shave fennel very thin on a mandolin, or use a vegetable peeler. Combine the fennel with crab and parsley. Season the mixture with lemon juice, olive oil and salt.

Roasted Cauliflower with Creamy Feta and 'Angry Sauce'

This robust cauliflower dish, the first recipe to appear in the series of weekly columns that became this cookbook, perfectly demonstrates the challenges of capturing a dynamic dining scene: By the time the series ended, Reid Henninger had left Edmund's Oast, and Bob Cook (featured elsewhere in this book) was in charge of its kitchen. But the precise flavor of July 2016 lives on here.

RECIPE BY Reid Henninger

1 whole head of cauliflower	1 cup marinated feta cheese, creamy	1 bunch of mint, chopped
Melted butter for pan-roasting	texture (Henninger likes the	1 bunch of parsley, chopped
Angry Sauce	version sold at goat.sheep.cow)	

Directions:

Blanch the whole head of cauliflower, untrimmed, in heavily salted boiling water. Cut into quarters and dry.

Pan-roast cauliflower cut sides down, basting with butter.

Smear creamy feta on serving plate, top with cauliflower and cover with Angry Sauce, mint and parsley.

ANGRY SAUCE

3½ ounces anchovy paste	2⅓ cups Calabrian chile, pureed (see	2 tablespoons sugar
1¼ cups white wine	cook's note)	2¼ tablespoons Red Boat fish sauce,
½ cup shallot, sliced thin	1⅓ cups Calabrian chile oil (see	or a fish sauce of choice
1 cup garlic, sliced thin	cook's note)	Salt, to taste
3 tablespoons picked thyme	1⅓ cups olive oil	Lemon juice, to taste
3 tablespoons picked rosemary	1 cup Champagne vinegar	

Directions:

Reduce anchovy and white wine by half. Combine remaining ingredients for sauce (through fish sauce) in mixing bowl. Add wine and anchovy reduction. Adjust with salt and lemon juice to taste.

COOK'S NOTE:

Calabrian chiles are Italian chiles celebrated for their complex, slightly fruity flavor. They're frequently sold jarred. If you can't find Calabrian chiles, use bottled cherry peppers.

WADE SPEES

Fish and Grits with Chraimeh Sauce

Like most of the dishes on the menu at Butcher & Bee, this fish preparation features a collision of local ingredients and Middle Eastern traditions. Here, the latter is represented by chraimeh, a sweet and spicy sauce associated with Tripolitan Jews.

RECIPE BY Chelsey Conrad

GRITS

3 cups water
4 tablespoons butter
1 cup of your favorite grits
1 cup heavy cream
3 tablespoons salt
2 tablespoons ground black pepper

Directions:

Bring water and butter to a boil in a medium saucepan and gradually whisk in grits, stirring constantly. Reduce heat to medium low and continue to stir constantly until grits begin to thicken, about 3 to 5 minutes. Reduce heat to low and cover. Let grits cook slowly over the course of an hour, stirring occasionally until tender. Season with cream, salt and pepper. Set aside until ready to serve.

CHRAIMEH

½ cup extra-virgin olive oil
1 yellow onion, diced
5 cloves of garlic, minced
1 jalapeno, minced
3 tablespoons caraway, dry toasted and ground
2 tablespoons sweet paprika
1 tablespoon ground cumin
1 tablespoon cayenne pepper
3 tablespoons salt
2 (28-ounce) cans whole tomatoes in juice
¼ cup fresh lemon juice

Directions:

Heat the olive oil over medium-high heat in a large Dutch oven, then saute onion, garlic and jalapeno until translucent and light brown, about 5 minutes. Add all spices and fry for 1 minute until fragrant. Add the canned tomatoes to the pot and use a spoon to crush tomatoes into bite-size pieces. Reduce heat and simmer for 30 minutes or until slightly thickened. Remove from heat; add the lemon juice and season to taste.

FISH

4 (5-ounce) fillets of your favorite fish, preferably a firmer fish such as swordfish, grouper or mahi-mahi
Salt
Ground white pepper
3 tablespoons oil
1 cup Chraimeh sauce, plus more for serving

WADE SPEES

Directions:

Preheat oven to 350 degrees. Pat fish fillets dry with a paper towel and season generously with salt and white pepper on both sides. Heat oil in a large saute pan over high heat until oil begins to smoke. Carefully set the fish fillets into the hot saute pan and saute until deep golden brown (about 4 minutes.) Gently turn each fillet over using tongs and spoon 1 cup of chraimeh sauce into the pan around the fish fillets. Pan roast the fish until just done, about 3 to 5 minutes, depending on the thickness of fillets.

PEPPERS + GARNISHES

1 pound of your favorite sweet peppers, such as padron, shishito, bell or banana

3 tablespoons chopped cilantro
Lemon, for zesting

Directions:

Lightly char the peppers whole on a grill pan, gas burner or outdoor grill. Allow to cool to the touch then slice into ringlets. Another delicious variation is sauteing sliced peppers.

To plate the fish and grits, spoon some grits onto each plate and create a well with the back of your spoon. Fill the well with a spoonful or two of warm chraimeh sauce and place a cooked fish fillet over the top. Top with another spoonful of sauce and a pile of sliced peppers. Zest a little lemon rind over each plate and garnish with the chopped cilantro.

Green Chile Corn Pudding

Considering how many cows Lewis Barbecue clears each week, the peninsula restaurant seems like an unlikely source for a stupendous vegetarian recipe. But this is Lewis' corn pudding, a dish that rivals the pitmaster's beef ribs and brisket in the acclaim category. Its fleecy texture and subtle chile flavor make the cheesed-up pudding suitable for just about any occasion, including Thanksgiving.

RECIPE BY John Lewis

- ¼ cup chopped roasted Hatch green chiles (about 2 or 3 chiles) (available at Whole Foods and other stores)
- ½ pound frozen corn kernels, pureed
- ¼ cup all-purpose flour
- ¼ cup yellow cornmeal

- 2 tablespoons granulated sugar
- 1 tablespoon kosher salt
- ½ teaspoon baking powder
- ¼ teaspoon granulated garlic
- 3 large eggs
- ⅔ cup heavy cream

- ½ cup mild cheddar cheese cut into ½-inch cubes
- ¾ cup corn kernels, freshly cut (1 ear of corn)
- 2 tablespoons butter
- ¼ cup shredded mild cheddar cheese

Directions:

Roast the Hatch green chiles over a hot open flame until the skins blacken and separate (about 4-5 minutes each side.) Place the roasted chiles in a sealable plastic bag and allow them to steam in their own heat for 1 hour. Peel the skins and remove the seeds. In a food processor, roughly chop the chiles.

Defrost the frozen corn kernels and chop in a food processor until pureed.

Combine the flour, yellow cornmeal, granulated sugar, salt, baking powder and granulated garlic in a mixing bowl. Blend together until homogeneous.

In a separate mixing bowl, beat the eggs and whisk in the heavy cream. Add the frozen corn puree, chopped and roasted Hatch green chiles, cubed mild cheddar cheese and fresh corn kernels. Pour the dry ingredients into the wet ingredients. Whisk together until homogeneous. Place a medium-sized cast-iron pan in the oven. Preheat oven to 375 degrees.

Take the heated cast-iron pan out of the oven and add the butter. Allow butter to heat until foaming and milk solids are lightly toasted. Be sure to allow the butter to fully coat the bottom.

Pour corn pudding batter into the hot cast-iron pan with foaming butter. Sprinkle the shredded mild cheddar cheese on the batter and return to the oven.

Cook for 30 minutes. The cheese should be nicely browned and the pudding should be set, but not firm in the center. Allow to rest for 5 minutes and serve.

GRACE BEAHM ALFORD

Off the Peninsula

Crab Cakes

The 'Wich Doctor is generally associated with pizza and sandwiches, but Butler doesn't neglect the Folly Beach restaurant's proximity to the ocean. Butler developed these crab cakes for a Vietnamese brunch menu offered exclusively on weekends.

RECIPE BY Jeff Butler

1 pound lump crab meat
¼ pound Virginia ham, finely diced
2 large eggs, lightly beaten
4 tablespoons all-purpose flour

2 tablespoons sweetened condensed milk
2 cups cold cooked jasmine rice (or any long-grain white rice)

1 cup plain dried breadcrumbs
Vegetable oil for frying

Directions:

Combine crab, ham, eggs, flour, condensed milk and rice in a large mixing bowl. Blend well with hands. Pour breadcrumbs on shallow plate.

Form crab mixture into patties about 2.5 inches in diameter. Press each side into breadcrumbs to coat. Continue until all of the mixture is formed into patties. Fry at 534 degrees for approximately 3 minutes. Drain on sheet lined with paper towels. Serve with the sauce.

THE SAUCE

½ cup water
½ cup white vinegar
1 cup brown sugar

¼ teaspoon salt
1 large cucumber
1 medium shallot, thinly sliced

1 red jalapeno (or other hot pepper of choice), seeded and diced

Directions:

Combine water, vinegar and sugar in a small saucepan over medium heat. Bring to a boil, stirring occasionally. Stir in salt, return to boil and cook 2 minutes, stirring occasionally. Reduce heat and cook at light heat until sauce reduces and thickens slightly (about 10 minutes.) Cool to room temperature.

Peel cucumber. Cut in half lengthwise. Scrape out seeds and dice. Put cucumber, shallot and chile in a bowl and pour cooled sauce over them. Mix well. Set aside.

WADE SPEES

Frogmore Stew

Ben Moise has been cooking Frogmore stew since the early 1980s, when he prepared a potful for the Heritage Golf Tournament at Hilton Head. He followed a recipe given to him by the late state Sen. Jimmy Waddell of Port Royal, and he still sticks to it.

That means no potatoes: Moise believes they make the shrimp harder to peel, and he's not fond of doubling up on starch. But to enhance stew eaters' corn enjoyment, he likes to put two melted sticks of butter and one-half teaspoon each of salt and Old Bay in a squeeze bottle. That way, diners can butter and hold their plates at the same time.

RECIPE BY Ben Moise

Old Bay seasoning
2½ pounds shrimp
(about 5 ounces per person)

2½ pounds kielbasa sausage
(about 5 ounces per person)

12 (3-inch) frozen corn "cobbettes"
(do not thaw prior to using)

Directions:

Fill a large pot with a strainer insert with approximately twice the volume of water as the volume of ingredients. It is essential to use a high-pressure regulator for the gas burner to bring the water rapidly back up to boil after cold ingredients have been added to the pot. To the water, add two handfuls of Old Bay and bring the pot to a boil. When the pot comes to a boil, add the sausage and the corn. Return to boil; cook for 8 minutes. Add the shrimp to the pot and cook for 2½ minutes, regardless of whether water is boiling. Pull the strainer and drain. Pour into serving container and sprinkle with more Old Bay. Serve with pickled coleslaw, seafood dipping sauce, butter and appropriate adult beverages.

PICKLED COLESLAW

1 red cabbage
1 green cabbage
2 large carrots
1 medium white onion

2 cloves garlic
Ginger root
1 teaspoon salt
1 teaspoon sugar

½ teaspoon black pepper
½ cup olive oil
½ cup vinegar

Directions:

Chop cabbages and place into a bowl. Skin carrots and cut them into bits; add to cabbage. Chop onion and add to cabbage mix. Grate garlic and 2-inch knob of ginger into a pot. Add salt, sugar and pepper. Mix in olive oil and vinegar; simmer for 5 minutes. Bring to a rapid boil and pour through a strainer onto cabbage mix. Toss well. Refrigerate for 2-3 hours before serving, tossing frequently.

GRACE BEAHM ALFORD

SEAFOOD DIPPING SAUCE

4 cups ketchup
½ cup ground horseradish

2 tablespoons Worcestershire sauce
4 tablespoons hot sauce

1 cup lemon juice or cider vinegar

Directions:

Mix together all ingredients.

Heirloom Bean Stew

 One of the defining features of the current Charleston restaurant scene is influence that extends far beyond the Lowcountry. Philosophies and techniques birthed here are carried to other cities by visiting chefs and veterans of local kitchens.

Jeremiah Langhorne of Washington, D.C.'s The Dabney, for example, was formerly McCrady's chef de cuisine. He provided this recipe in advance of his first trip back to Charleston: It features Sea Island Purple Cape Beans, which producer Anson Mills describes as dark, woodsy and velvet-like; if you can't find them, use your favorite heirloom beans instead.

RECIPE BY Jeremiah Langhorne

HEIRLOOM BEAN STEW

1 pound Anson Mills purple cape beans
6 cups water
2 large onions
6 medium-size carrots
1 stalk (head) celery
1 head garlic
1 turnip or 4-5 baby turnips

1 large kohlrabi
6-8 ounces country ham scraps or salt pork
1 bunch parsley
1 bunch chives
2 lemons
2 tablespoons extra-virgin olive oil
2 quarts chicken stock or broth

4 bay leaves
6 sprigs thyme
½ pound spinach or other favorite green
½ pound butter
2 tablespoons cider vinegar
Hot sauce, to taste
Salt and pepper, to taste

Directions:

Soak beans in water overnight.

Dice the onion. Chop carrots and celery. Peel and mince garlic.

Peel turnips and kohlrabi. Cut into uniform pieces. Chop ham.

Chop parsley and chives. Mix most of the parsley with chives, reserving a few leaves for garnish.

Cut lemons into sixths and remove seeds.

Place a heavy-bottom pot on the stove over medium heat. Add pork, slowly rendering out fat. Add olive oil and onions.

Once the onions have sweated down, add the celery and half of the carrots. Add stock, beans, bay leaves and thyme.

When the beans are almost totally creamy, add remaining carrots, garlic, turnips, kohlrabi, parsley-chive mixture and spinach to the pot. Stir in the butter and emulsify. Continue cooking until the beans become totally creamy.

Season with lemon sixths, parsley, cider vinegar, hot sauce, salt and pepper. Set stew aside.

GRILLED TROUT

6 (5-ounce) portions of freshest fish available (it doesn't have to be trout)

Extra-virgin olive oil
1 lemon

Salt and pepper, to taste

Directions:

Turn on grill or preheat oven to 400 degrees if using a cast-iron pan for cooking.

Make sure your grill is on and you have even red coals; or if it's gas, 400 degrees. Lightly oil the fish portions and lay them skin-down on the grill or in the oven. Do not touch fish for at least 3 minutes.

If you can't easily lift the fish off its cooking surface, allow it to cook longer. When it's ready, flip over portions; cook for 1-2 minutes. Remove fish from grill or oven. Squeeze lemon over fish. Season with salt and pepper.

To assemble:

Divide the stew into 6 bowls and place 1 portion of fish atop each serving. Remove bay leaves.

Greens and Brussels Sprouts Salad

There are greens galore in this roasted Brussels sprouts salad, but it gains color diversity from corn and carrots. That's especially true if you follow Blake McCormick's lead and use rainbow carrots: They taste just like common orange carrots, but their purple, red and yellow hues signal that they contain different sets of nutrients.

RECIPE BY Blake McCormick

1 pound Brussels sprouts
2 cups brown butter vinaigrette (see recipe)
2 shucked ears of corn

Salt and pepper
2 large carrots
2 ounces pickled Fresno chiles
¾ pound arugula

½ pound Tuscan kale
⅛ cup pine nuts
2 Honeycrisp apples
⅓ cup crumbled feta (preferably goat)

Directions:

Preheat oven to 400 degrees. Thoroughly rinse Brussels sprouts in cold water. Remove any outer leaves that are wilted. Trim the very end of stems, taking care to remove as little of the stem as possible. Halve and then quarter sprouts, aiming to keep the segments intact. Set aside.

Make the brown butter vinaigrette.

Remove kernels from ears of corn. Spread them on a well-oiled sheet pan; season with salt and pepper; place pan in oven, stirring occasionally. Roast kernels until golden and slightly charred. Remove and set aside to cool. Do not turn off the oven. Peel carrots and slice them finely, ideally on a Japanese mandolin. Reserve the slices in cool water.

Dice the Fresno chiles. Clean and dry the arugula and kale. Cut the kale into fine strips.

Place pine nuts on an oiled sheet pan, and toast in oven until golden brown, about 8-10 minutes. Set aside to cool.

Wash the apples; slice on a mandolin. Set aside.

Heat an ungreased cast-iron pan over high heat until smoking slightly. While the pan heats, combine all of the fruits and vegetables except for the Brussels sprouts in a large bowl. Season with salt and pepper.

Add Brussels sprouts to pan by the handful, creating an even layer. Do not stir. Once the sprouts have charred, flip them over. Turn down the heat if the sprouts are burning or there's too much smoke.

Once the sprouts are evenly cooked, reduce heat to low and add just enough brown butter vinaigrette to coat the sprouts, 1 ounce at a time. Stir the sprouts until completely dressed. Turn off heat. Sprinkle sprouts with sea salt.

Dress salad with remaining brown butter vinaigrette. Be sure to not overdress. Toss to coat. Divide the salad between two plates or bowls. Portion sprouts evenly atop the two salads. Sprinkle feta over the salads, and eat immediately.

WADE SPEES

BROWN BUTTER VINAIGRETTE

3 sticks butter (browned, will yield ¾ fluid ounce)

¾ cup sherry vinegar
1 shallot, chopped

2 tablespoons Dijon mustard
¾ cup extra-virgin olive oil

Directions:

In heavy-bottomed pot, slowly melt butter over medium heat, gently stirring with spatula. Do not whisk or stir vigorously. Butter solids will slowly start to separate, and butter will begin to foam; reduce heat if needed so the butter doesn't burn.

Cook until the butter has a nutty aroma and has progressed from a lemony yellow to a golden tan.

Remove from heat and gently pass through a fine strainer into a heat-proof bowl. Set aside. In a blender, combine sherry vinegar, shallots and mustard.

Turn speed up to medium-high. Slowly pour in olive oil, then add brown butter, allowing it to emulsify. Blend until combined. Season with salt and pepper.

Field Pea Falafel

"The idea for a Southern take on falafel always lingered in the back of my mind," Stewart says. "Now during the summer we substitute local field peas or butterbeans for the traditional chickpea. We serve it as a po-boy or with a nice tomato, cucumber and feta salad."

Stewart adds that cooks shouldn't be put off by the number of steps in this food processor-based recipe. "The actual falafel base can be made up to a week in advance, and then fried immediately before your gathering," he promises.

RECIPE BY Chris Stewart

2 tablespoons cumin seeds	2 tablespoons extra-virgin olive oil	2 cups all-purpose flour
¼ cup garlic cloves (about 10 cloves)	1 lemon, juiced and strained	2 eggs
4 cups cooked field peas, well-salted	2 teaspoons freshly ground black pepper	1 cup milk
1 cup chopped green onion, or one half of a medium onion	5 tablespoons water	Panko bread crumbs
		2 quarts vegetable oil

Directions:

Add cumin seeds to bowl of a full-size food processor. Run for about 30 seconds, until seeds are cracked and bruised. Next, add garlic and run until minced. Add peas, green onion, olive oil, lemon juice and black pepper to food processor. Run until mixture is thoroughly combined and minced. At this point, mixture should be very dry; the desired final consistency is smooth and dry, but when pressed, the base should form a ball. To achieve that consistency, gradually add water, one tablespoon at a time.

Shape the falafel base into golf ball-sized balls. Use three medium-sized bowls to create a three-step breading station. In first bowl, place flour. In second bowl, combine eggs and milk; whisk to combine. In third bowl, place bread crumbs. Take each falafel ball down the bowl assembly line, dipping first in flour, then egg mixture and then finally in bread crumbs. Line up the falafel balls on a baking sheet for easy frying.

Heat oil to 350 degrees in a large pot over medium heat. (An even oil temperature is key to frying. A clip-on candy/fry thermometer should be kept in the pot at all times, and the temperature should register at least 300 degrees during frying process.) Using tongs and working in small batches (about 3 balls per session), fry balls for about 3 minutes, or until golden brown and warm at the center. Remove from oil, using tongs and transfer to a paper towel-lined baking sheet. Finished falafels can be held in a 200-degree oven while you finish the frying process.

Feel free to season the fried falafel with salt and freshly ground black pepper as your taste buds desire.

GRACE BEAHM ALFORD

Collard Greens

S iegel of Home Team BBQ wants to make sure everyone gets their fill of smoked meat, even if they're eating vegetables. His recipe for greens comes by its porky, smoky flavor with the help of smoked hocks and shoulder.

RECIPE BY Aaron Siegel

1 gallon water	½ cup kosher salt	½ pound smoked pork shoulder,
3 cups cider vinegar	2 to 3 shoulder bones or smoked	chopped or pulled
¼ cup hot sauce	ham hocks	2 pound collard greens, stems
½ cup brown sugar		removed, cut in 2-inch strips

Directions:

Bring water to a simmer. Add cider vinegar, hot sauce, brown sugar and kosher salt. Add bones or ham hocks for flavor and simmer for 25 minutes. Add smoked pork and greens. Simmer lightly for 2 to 3 hours or until tender.

GRACE BEAHM ALFORD

Soft-Shell Crab Ramen

I n 2017, excitement over the soft-shell crab harvest was muted, perhaps because Charleston's most enthusiastic eaters were plumb worn out: Because of irregular weather, crabs arrived on the heels of the Charleston Wine + Food Festival.

But no matter what the calendar says, softies are still delicious. For this preparation, which recognizes the weird concurrence of cold nights and molting crabs, Lagace combined the popular seafood with ever-trendy ramen.

RECIPE BY Matthew Lagace

SOY RAMEN BROTH

¼ cup soy sauce
1 cup chicken stock
1 cup beef stock

1 clove garlic, smashed
¼ shallot, roughly chopped
½ ounce ginger, peeled and roughly chopped

¼ jalapeno, seeds removed, roughly chopped

Directions:
   Add all ingredients to a stockpot. Boil until mixture is reduced by ¼. Strain and set aside.

SOFT-SHELL CRAB

⅓ cup black & white sesame seeds
2 watermelon radishes
6 scallions
2 quarts rice bran oil
4 cups rice flour

2½ cups ice-cold soda water
3 egg yolks
⅔ cup sesame oil
2 cups sake
Salt and white pepper to taste

6 soft-shell crabs
6 ounces ramen or udon noodles
6 eggs
⅓ ounce tobikko wasabi
1 cup microgreens

Directions:
   Preheat oven to 350 degrees.
   Spread seeds on a baking sheet; toast in oven for 8-10 minutes. Set aside.
   Clean radishes. Slice thinly and cut into matchsticks; reserve radishes in a small bowl filled with water.
   Clean scallions. Coat with oil; salt and pepper. Char in a grill pan, or briefly broil until charred. Set aside.
   Heat rice bran oil in a large pot to 375 degrees.
   In a large bowl, blend rice flour; soda water; egg yolks; sesame oil; sake; salt and pepper.

Dip one cleaned crab in tempura batter; fry until golden brown. Repeat with each crab. Set aside.
   To assemble one serving, boil 4 ounces of ramen broth in a sauté pan. Cook 1 ounce of noodles until soft. While the noodles are cooking, fry one egg, sunny side-up. Place broth and noodles in a serving bowl. Top with crab, egg, a few radishes, 1 scallion, approximately 2 teaspoons of wasabi and 2 tablespoons of microgreens. Sprinkle sesame seeds over dish.
   Repeat for each additional serving.

WADE SPEES

Roasted Butternut Squash

"**P**ersonally if I could, I would only cook vegetables and fish," Wang says. "Those I think have always been my strong point." Despite Wang's wishes, his customers tend to order "chicken, chicken, chicken, chicken."

This dish is a fine illustration of what poultry lovers are missing. Wang likes to sprinkle the roasted squash with togarashi, a Japanese chile-based seasoning blend available from Asian markets and spice stores, but it's OK to omit that last step. And if you don't have the equipment to smoke sour cream (which Wang swears is easier than it sounds), plain sour cream works, too.

RECIPE BY Shuai Wang

1 medium butternut squash, quartered and seeded
Olive oil
½ cup sweet white miso
1 cup light soy sauce
⅓ cup honey

⅓ cup freshly squeezed lemon juice
¼ cup cornstarch
¼ cup full-fat sour cream, lightly smoked
1 cup chives, finely sliced (roughly equivalent to an average bunch)

¼ cup toasted pecans, chopped
½ cup crumbled feta or ricotta salata (goat milk feta preferred)
Togarashi spice (optional)

Directions:

Preheat oven to 350 degrees. Toss the quartered and cleaned squash with just enough olive oil to coat. Rub down squash with miso paste, making sure every piece is evenly coated.

Place the squash wedges on a baking pan lined with parchment paper, skin side down. Using the oven's middle rack, roast the squash until tender, about 30 minutes or so. Remove the squash from the oven before it begins to brown, allowing it to cool.

While squash is cooking, add the light soy sauce, honey and lemon juice to a small sauce pot over medium heat. Whisk lightly just until the honey has dissolved, then bring to a light simmer; if the ponzu sauce boils, it will taste burnt.

Whisk together cornstarch and water;

it should have the consistency of heavy cream. Slowly drizzle the cornstarch slurry into the ponzu, and continue whisking until it thickens. The ponzu should be clear and no thicker than heavy cream. If the sauce is thin and cloudy and not thick, the cornstarch is still cooking. Chill the mixture to room temperature and set aside for later.

If you have a smoker or grill, heat it to 260 degrees and season with hickory chips. Wait until the smoke is rolling. Put your sour cream in oven-safe cookware and let it smoke for 10 minutes. When it is done, immediately put the container on ice to cool down.

Preheat the oven to 500 degrees. Place as many squash quarters as you want to serve in the oven to reheat; tightly wrapped, the rest will keep in the refrigerator for a week. Using

WADE SPEES

the middle rack, cook squash until slightly charred on the outside. Remove from oven and cool slightly.

Meanwhile, spoon some of the smoked cream on to an oval plate and spread lightly around center; cover the rest of the plate with a light layer of ponzu sauce.

Place the roasted squash quarters on top of the sauce. Garnish the top with chives, pecans and cheese; finish with light layer of togarashi, if using.

Edisto Shrimp and Blue Crab Toast

From his perch on Edisto Island, Brandon Rushing has access to impeccably fresh seafood, including the shrimp featured aboard this trendy toast. If you haven't made the trip to Edisto lately, shrimp delivered to other South Carolina docks work just as well in this recipe. Just rename accordingly.

RECIPE BY Brandon Rushing

SHRIMP AND CRAB TOAST

1 pound small Edisto shrimp, poached and chopped
3 whole eggs
8 ounces mayonnaise
1½ tablespoons Creole mustard
1½ tablespoons Worcestershire sauce

1½ tablespoons Old Bay seasoning
1 teaspoon Tabasco sauce
1 cup panko bread crumbs
½ bunch chives, chopped
1 teaspoon black pepper
2 lemons, juiced

1 pound fresh jumbo lump crab meat
7 thick slices of sourdough bread
7 tablespoons butter

Directions:

Combine all of the ingredients in a large bowl except for the crab meat, bread and butter. Once well combined, gently fold in the crab meat.

Heat a large cast-iron skillet over medium heat. Spread a thick layer of shrimp and crab mixture atop each slice of sourdough bread. Add butter to the pan. Once the butter has melted, add open-face sandwiches, shrimp side down. Cook until golden brown; flip and repeat.

ASPARAGUS SALAD

1 bunch large asparagus
6 ears of sweet white corn

1 pint cherry tomatoes, halved
Salt and pepper

Tomato tarragon vinaigrette

Directions:

Shave the raw asparagus with a potato peeler into thin ribbons and place into a large bowl. Shuck kernels from the ears of corn into the same bowl. Add tomatoes. Toss in desired amount of vinaigrette. Adjust seasoning.

MICHAEL PRONZATO

TOMATO TARRAGON VINAIGRETTE

½ pound oven-roasted tomatoes
½ cup Champagne vinegar
1 tablespoon Dijon mustard

1 tablespoon tarragon, chopped
¼ teaspoon salt
¼ teaspoon black pepper

½ cup olive oil

Directions:

Roast tomatoes in a 500-degree oven for 7 minutes, and then cool. When tomatoes are cool, add to a blender along with vinegar, mustard, tarragon, salt and pepper. Turn blender on. Slowly drizzle in olive oil to emulsify. Adjust seasoning to taste.

To assemble:

Slice each piece of toast into three pieces. Drizzle lightly with portion of the remaining vinaigrette and top with a generous amount of asparagus salad.

Ceviche

After a year of serving entrees, Congress in Mount Pleasant reinvented itself as an all-tapas restaurant. This refreshing ceviche verde from Ciaburri was added to the regular menu, along with small plates such as achiote pork tacos and scallop aguachile.

RECIPE BY Mark Ciaburri

2 pounds shrimp, peeled and deveined	½ bunch plus 1 tablespoon of cilantro	1 avocado
⅓ cup whole black peppercorns	¾ cup fat-free Greek yogurt	4 tomatillos, finely diced
8 limes	1 clove garlic, smashed	½ habanero chile, thinly sliced
4 lemons	1 teaspoon honey	¼ pineapple, grilled & diced
4 oranges	1 tablespoon grapeseed oil	Salt and pepper
		Extra-virgin olive oil

Directions:

Boil water in pot large enough to hold shrimp. Partially cook the shrimp with black peppercorns for 1 minute, then immediately submerge in an ice bath to shock. Juice 4 limes, along with lemons and oranges, into a large bowl. Once the shrimp are chilled, marinate in the citrus juice for at least 1 hour.

Combine the juice of 2 limes with 1 tablespoon of cilantro, yogurt, garlic, honey and grapeseed oil in a blender and puree. Add avocado and blend until smooth. Season with salt and pepper to taste.

Toss marinated shrimp with avocado dressing, tomatillos, habanero and pineapple, as well as the juice of two remaining limes. Season to taste. Garnish with cilantro leaves and olive oil; serve with tortilla chips.

WADE SPEES

Okra Soup

"The only constant is change," is a cliché that's routinely slapped on a dining scene that welcomes new restaurants on a weekly basis. But it's perhaps more accurate to say Charleston's constant is okra soup.

Although gumbo's Lowcountry cousin is rarely referenced in the city's fanciest restaurants, it's still served in homes and affordable luncheonettes, which is why Dennis, a personal chef and caterer, believed it deserved a page in this book. Dennis' version of the traditional soup is made with shrimp, rather than beef, which usually governs the tomato broth. But disagreeing about tradition is a local constant too.

RECIPE BY Benjamin "B.J." Dennis

½ pound of smoked meat, such as pork or turkey (optional)	5 cloves garlic	½ pound fresh butterbeans, shelled
2 pounds fresh tomatoes, diced, or one 28-ounce can of diced tomatoes	1 hot pepper	1 small onion
	1 bay leaf	Salt
	3 to 4 thyme sprigs	½ pound of shrimp, cleaned
	1 pound okra	

Directions:

If using smoked meat, add it to pot with tomato, garlic, hot pepper, bay leaf and thyme. Pour water over meat to just cover. Cook over medium-high heat until meat is tender.

Slice okra into half-inch pieces. Dice onion. Add okra, butterbeans and onions to pot; cook until okra is tender, approximately 10-15 minutes.

Salt shrimp and add to pot. Cook shrimp for 2-3 minutes. Salt to taste throughout cooking process. Remove bay leaf. Serve with rice.

For a vegan version of the soup, coat the bottom of a pot with olive oil. Add tomato, garlic, hot pepper, bay leaf and thyme and saute for 5 minutes. Add 3-4 cups of water. Bring soup to boil, then reduce heat to simmer for 20 minutes. Remove bay leaf before serving.

WADE SPEES

Index